COUNSELLING SKILLS
TRAINING

COUNSELLING SKILLS TRAINING

A Sourcebook of
Activities for Trainers

PHILIP BURNARD

KOGAN
PAGE

First published in 1992

Apart from any fair dealing for the purposes of research or private study, or
criticism or review, as permitted under the Copyright, Designs and Patents
Act, 1988, this publication may only be reproduced, stored or transmitted, in
any form or by any means, with the prior permission in writing of the
publishers, or in the case of reprographic reproduction in accordance with the
terms of licences issued by the Copyright Licensing Agency. Enquiries
concerning reproduction outside those terms should be sent to the publishers
at the undermentioned address:

Kogan Page Limited
120 Pentonville Road
London N1 9JN

© Philip Burnard, 1992

British Library Cataloguing in Publication Data

A CIP record for this book is available from the British Library.

ISBN 0 7494 0828 6

Typeset by DP Photosetting, Aylesbury, Bucks
Printed and bound in Great Britain by
Biddles Ltd, Guildford and Kings Lynn

Contents

List of activities

Introduction

More and more people need counselling skills and yet there is little training material in this field. This book is for anyone who is concerned with training people in counselling skills. It contains theory as well as ideas for practice. Essentially, though, it is a sourcebook of activities to be used in training courses and workshops. It is based on the research and literature on counselling and grounded in my own experience as a teacher, trainer and researcher in the field. As far as possible, I have tried to avoid a particular theoretical 'position'. It is easy to get caught in traps about which theory is best or about which style of counselling is most effective. Instead, I have tried to keep controversial theory to a minimum and to invite readers to judge for themselves what does and does not work.

WHO THE BOOK IS FOR

Counselling has a wide range of applications. It is used by managers and by health care workers, by teachers and by voluntary workers. This manual is for *anyone* who wants to teach others to enhance their counselling skills. A short list of those people would include those in:

- business and administration training;
- management training;
- further and higher education;

- workshop facilitation;
- the human potential field;
- post-basic education and training;
- the health professions;
- customer relations training;
- personnel training;
- public relations;
- schools, further and higher education.

WHAT IS IN THE BOOK

The early chapters of this book identify some of the theoretical aspects of counselling skills training. Chapter 1 is about counselling, itself. Chapter 2 identifies the elements that go to make up counselling skills training, while chapter 3 identifies ways of evaluating counselling skills courses and workshops. To evaluate is to improve the next time round. Counselling is an evolving field of study and of practice. It seems to me essential to evaluate continually what we are doing. Chapters 4 and 5 offer a series of checklists which cover most aspects of the process of setting up counselling skills training. They offer a useful and 'shorthand' method of identifying what you need to think about when planning and running a course or workshop. Chapter 6 focuses on experiential learning: the process of learning by doing. Counselling can never be taught simply through lecturing or even only through discussion. At some point, people have to try out what they have been talking about. Experiential learning methods offer a practical way of learning from direct experience. Chapter 7 is an introduction to the exercises contained in the second part of the book and offers full details of how to make best use of the activities.

The final chapters contain detailed descriptions of 80 activities for developing counselling skills. Many of them include handouts that can be photocopied and used in group settings. Also, they can be modified to suit *your* particular needs and preferences. This is important. Not all trainers and not all trainees like all exercises and activities. In some of the research that I have done, I have found, for instance, that quite a number of people do not like role play. Others enjoy it and find it useful. In considering the activities that you want to use, you should bear in mind your own preferences and those of your trainees.

The activities contained in Part II cover a wide range of counselling skills:

- Listening-skills activities;
- Empathy-building activities;
- Information and advice-giving activities;
- Facilitation activities;
- Problem-solving activities;
- Coping with feelings;
- Evaluation activities;
- Counsellor-development activities.

The book is for use with a very varied trainee group. The sorts of people with whom the activities might be used include:

- students;
- managers;
- researchers;
- colleagues;
- health-care clients;
- residents;
- customers;
- patients;

and many others.

Labels are always difficult. To keep things simple, I have used the term 'trainer' to describe the person who is running the counselling course or workshop. I have used the term 'trainee' to describe the person who attends such courses and workshops. I appreciate that other people will prefer words such as 'facilitator' and 'client'. There are no easy answers in this sensitive area. It might be a good idea to discuss with any given group what they prefer to call themselves.

HOW TO USE THE BOOK

This is a book to be used as well as read. Indeed, you may decide that you don't need to read all of it. Or you may read sections of it at different times. If you are already a trainer then you may want to turn straight to the second section and use some of the activities.

I feel that it is important to see this as a *user manual,* rather than just a book. It is something to be written in, marked, taken into classrooms and referred to. As I have indicated, above, you are free to photocopy relevant pages for use in courses and workshops. Please include the copyright note appearing at the foot of such pages when copying.

I hope that you enjoy using the activities in this book and that you adapt them to suit your own circumstances. Some of the most useful activities are the ones that you make up yourself – often on the spur of the moment. All the activities here have been used in a variety of workshops and courses and with a range of trainee groups. They all *work* as activities. No guarantee can, of course, be given that they will automatically turn people into effective counsellors, but they *will* help people to reflect on their behaviour. Becoming aware of what we do and how we do it is the first stage in the process of becoming an effective counsellor – and we are all in that state of 'becoming'. Few people, I imagine, would claim to be experts: most of us are still learning how to help other people. And so it should be. Humility in counselling and helping other people is a fundamental ingredient.

PART I

SKILLS TRAINING

Chapter 1:

Counselling

AIMS OF THE CHAPTER

This chapter discusses the following aspects of counselling:

- definitions;
- applications;
- personal qualities of the counsellor;
- pitfalls and how to overcome them.

DEFINITIONS

Most of us have come across counselling in one form or another. This is the problem: the word is so familiar that lots of people have different ways of defining it. To some, it involves never asking direct questions. To others, it involves giving advice and making suggestions about how another person might help themselves. Yet others scorn such an idea and feel that it is always the recipient of counselling who identifies solutions to problems.

Here are some ways in which people have defined counselling:

Counselling is the means by which one person helps another through purposeful conversation.

Counselling involves a series of problem-solving interviews.

Counselling is a process in which two people meet to explore personal problems and to identify solutions.

Counselling is a method of identifying practical solutions to life or work-related problems.

There are certain factors that seem common to all or most of these definitions and about which many counsellors would agree. Definitions of counselling usually involve some or all of the following:

- two people are present;
- the process leads to action on the part of the client;
- the counsellor is a person who listens;
- the client can be trusted to find their own solutions;
- personal growth of the client usually occurs;
- resolution of problems is an expectation.

Some counsellors would add to this list and you may feel that there are things that *you* would add to it. This is an important aspect of counselling-skills training. A very early exercise in any counselling-skills workshop or course is one that involves exploring trainees' perceptions of counselling. It does not pay to be dogmatic on these issues. There is room for a variety of definitions. Having said that, there are also some things that counselling does *not* seem to be about. Counselling is not usually concerned with:

- advice-giving on the part of the counsellor;
- psychotherapy;
- treatment of severe mental illness;
- solving all life's problems.

Like all forms of talking, counselling has its limitations. It cannot solve all of the problems that life throws at us. In the end, too, we have to stop talking and *act*. What must not happen in counselling is merely that two people meet and talk and talk and talk... Counselling must always have a *practical* end. What people often fear most of all is changing. Often, people are happier to talk about how they might change than to do it; but, in the end, if counselling can be said to be effective, change on the part of the client is a vital element of the whole process.

THE ESSENTIAL ELEMENTS OF COUNSELLING

Two researchers and counselling theorists have attempted to identify the factors that are essential to the process of counselling. Fiedler asked a range of counsellors to say what they considered to be the ideal therapeutic relationship. The list that they compiled (Fiedler 1950) included:

- an empathic relationship;
- the counsellor and client relate well;
- the counsellor sticks closely to the client's problems;
- the client feels free to say what they like;
- an atmosphere of mutual trust and confidence exists;
- rapport is essential.

Some years later, Carl Rogers, father of client-centred counselling, developed that list and produced what Rogers was to call the 'necessary and sufficient conditions for therapeutic change' (Rogers 1957). He hypothesized that the following conditions had to be present if counselling was to be effective:

- two persons are in psychological contact;
- the first, the client, is in a state of incongruence, vulnerable and anxious;
- the second, the counsellor, is congruent or integrated in the relationship;
- the counsellor experiences unconditional regard for the client;
- the counsellor experiences an empathic understanding of the client's internal frame of reference and endeavours to communicate this experience to the client;
- the communication to the client of the counsellor's empathic

understanding and unconditional positive regard is to a minimal degree achieved.

In his description, Rogers used two key phrases: unconditional regard and empathic understanding. We return to these two characteristics later in this chapter. For now, though, it is worth considering the degree to which you feel both Fiedler's and Rogers' lists are true of counselling today. While the political, economic and social climates of the world have changed, it seems likely that the human element has stayed much the same. It is still important to meet another person on intimate terms. It is still necessary to feel listened to and understood and, most of all, it is important that people still have time for *relationships*. This is as true in business and management as it is in the helping professions and teaching – counselling has a wide and diverse range of applications.

APPLICATIONS

In some ways, counselling skills are just an extension of everyday, effective communication skills. However, there are important differences between ordinary conversations and counselling. Perhaps the most important difference lies in the fact that, in counselling, one person is the counsellor and the other the client. The counselling relationship is rarely an equal one. In counselling, there is nearly always an expectation that one person will talk about problems while the other listens. In an ordinary conversation, there is more freedom for interaction between the two parties. Usually, too, in such a conversation, there is a greater tendency to share experiences, to give each other advice and to make suggestions. In counselling, the emphasis, as we have seen, is usually on encouraging clients to make their own decisions based on their own assessment of what the 'problem' might be.

The possible range of counselling situations, however, is vast. Here are some examples of how counselling might be used in a variety of settings:

An employee in a large company makes an appointment to see a senior manager about possible career moves.

A student seeks out his personal tutor to discuss emotional problems which he perceives to be affecting his academic work.

A young girl talks to a community worker about fears she has about the possibility of being anorexic.

A community worker talks through a young man's fear that he is the subject of racial abuse.

A couple seek advice about their apparently failing marriage.

A middle-aged executive faces unemployment and wants to talk through the possible options that may or may not open up for her.

What is common to all these situations is that the person who is engaged in counselling begins by listening to the other person. An effective counsellor does not jump in with advice and suggestions but allows the other person to verbalize all aspects of their situation. Out of this verbalization begins to emerge a clearer picture of what the problem or problems might be. Then comes a stage in which both client and counsellor work out possible strategies for relieving or resolving the situation. We will explore the various stages of the counselling process in more detail, later in this chapter. At this stage, though, it is important to note that what typifies the counselling relationship most is the ability of the counsellor to listen and neither to judge nor to offer advice immediately. Often, the process of learning to be a counsellor is also a process of *un*learning. Many of us are programmed from an early point in our lives to offer our opinion on a subject or to make positive suggestions about what might be done about a particular situation. If you work in business or management, you may be trained to think in this way. If you work in further and higher education, your critical faculties might be organized in such a way as to try to spot illogicalities and to point them out to others. Counselling, however, entails the suspension of some of these 'normal' responses in favour of a much more accepting and giving role.

The immediate significance of all this is that the counselling-skills trainer needs to consider how to model this role in courses and workshops, for in counselling training, perhaps more than in many other sorts of teaching situations, the trainer must demonstrate the sorts of qualities that should be evident in the counselling practitioner. This personal aspect of counselling is another feature that marks it out from other business, educational and management functions. Before identifying both the stages of the counselling process and the skills that are involved, it is important to consider what personal qualities are needed in order to be an effective counsellor.

PERSONAL QUALITIES OF THE COUNSELLOR

All sorts of people become counsellors. They do so, as we have seen, in a wide range of settings. It would be ludicrous to assume that they all have the same personality profile or set of personal characteristics. On the other hand, if we reflect on the sort of people that *we* could talk to easily, we may find that we can agree, to some degree, on the personal qualities that should be present in all counsellors.

Before you read on, reflect for a few minutes on the sort of person that you would like to be counselled by. If possible, jot down the personal qualities that you would look for in such a person. Keep your jottings focused only on personal qualities. Do not list the skills that you would expect, nor the type of counselling that you would want to receive. Consider, too, running this sort of activity in your counselling skills workshops or courses. Once you have identified at least three qualities, read on.

A number of researchers in the counselling field have tried to identify the personal qualities that are necessary to effect therapeutic change in another person. Carkuff (1969) suggested that a climate of trust must be developed in counselling in which the following characteristics are present: *empathy, warmth, genuineness.* Carl Rogers (1967) added the following necessary qualities: *positive regard, concreteness.* Drawing from the considerable literature and research conducted in the field of counselling, the following other personal characteristics may be added: *a sense of humour, a sense of the tragic, self-awareness.*

Each of these is now discussed briefly. Further details of these and other qualities can be found in the literature on counselling and therapy and the reader is referred to these. Of particular note, are the following (see References on pp 304–5 for publication details):

C.R. Rogers, *Client-Centred Counselling*. The first book of its sort that highlighted what counselling might involve. A detailed book which offers both evidence from research reports and a great deal of useful theory about the nature and practice of counselling.

R. Nelson-Jones, *The Theory and Practice of Counselling Psychology*. A detailed account of almost all aspects of counselling. A book that is very strong on both the theory and the practice of counselling.

P. Burnard, *Counselling Skills for Health Professionals*. An introductory text which offers details of both the skills involved in counselling and the psychological theories that lie behind them.

Empathy

Empathy is the ability to stand in the other person's shoes – to see the world as they see it. In the end, we can never empathize completely. All we can do is try to drop our own preconceptions and really listen to the other person in order to try to enter their 'frame of reference'. We do not empathize if we constantly compare the other person's situation with our own. Empathy involves a certain 'forgetting of self' in order to give ourselves up to the other person. It is a quality that can be enhanced through training but also one that some have in greater abundance than others. It is an essential quality in counselling. Without some appreciation of the other person's world-view, we run the danger of moralizing, advising and of generally getting the wrong end of the stick. In the second part of this book, various activities are offered which help to enhance empathy.

Warmth

The idea of being 'warm' is a delicate one. One person's warmth is another person sickliness. How we define what a warm person might be like depends, to a large degree, on our personal experiences and preferences. On the other hand, it seems unlikely that a really 'cold' person would either want to be a counsellor or be very good at it. Being warm suggests an inherent interest in other people.

There are, of course, limitations here. If you are too warm, you risk smothering the other person; you also risk a dependence developing. The ideal, perhaps, is a warmth which shows that you are non-judgemental and genuinely interested in what the other person has to say, without 'taking over'. Warmth seems to be linked to a certain non-defensiveness. The person who is going to function as a counsellor may want to explore his or her own problems a little before setting up as a potential counsellor. The problem with *not* doing so is that such personal problems can come back to haunt you in the counselling relationship. If you have lots of personal issues sitting in the background then, if the client you are with has similar problems, you may find their difficulties reawakening your own. While no one can sort out all their life problems, counsellors should, at least, be prepared to face some of their own.

Genuineness

Both Rogers and Truax (1967) were at pains to point to the importance of genuineness in counselling. It is difficult to feign real interest in another person. You either have it or you don't. It is interesting to think about those people in public service who are trained to meet the public in a professional but friendly manner: hotel staff, airline operatives and fast-food chain employees are obvious examples. In none of these cases does it seem likely that you will confuse their 'public front' with true 'genuineness'. Being genuine in the counselling relationship is more than just the development of a certain list of behaviours. It is more a question of intent. If you are genuine, you intend to help or care for the other person.

We cannot be genuinely interested in all people at all times. It seems likely, though, that if you are not interested in this particular person, someone else will be. An interesting point for the counselling-skills trainer is this: what factors determine whether or not you *are* interested in another person? Consider this point for a moment.

> *Consider the sort of people that interest you and for whom you could be genuine. If you can, jot down the names of three or four such people. Now consider what it is about them that makes you feel genuine towards them. This activity can throw up your own interests, concerns and limitations. It is an activity that can be adapted for use in counselling-skills workshops and courses.*

Positive regard

Rogers (1967) coined the term 'unconditional positive regard' to describe one of what he called the 'necessary and sufficient conditions for therapeutic change' in the counselling relationship. Many of our relationships are conditional. We like others as long as they like us. We get on with people who treat us in a reasonable sort of way. Rogers claims that the counsellor's positive feelings for the client must not be conditional. He suggests that the counsellor should feel warmly disposed towards the other person *whatever* the client feels or says to the counsellor. This is an almost saintly position which is probably better thought of as an aim rather than as a likely reality.

On the other hand, it is important that a counsellor is broad minded and not prone to easy judgement of other people. Also, it is important that his or her general disposition towards others is positive. Clearly, a person who sees the worst in people is unlikely to make a very effective counsellor.

Concreteness

Concreteness is almost a skill. It is the ability to get to listen to what the other person is saying and to stick with what is being *said* rather than what is implied. The aim, here, is to adopt Sartre's (1955) view that 'things are as they appear to be'. That sums it up. The concrete counsellor accepts what the client says at face value and does not interpret or try to read between the lines. For the simple fact appears to be that we cannot know what another person 'really means': we must rely on that person's account of things. The concrete counsellor does not offer detailed psychological explanations of what the client is talking about but tries, instead, to get closer to what the client is trying to say. Here is an example of concreteness in practice:

I don't know. I just seem to get things sorted out and then all sorts of things happen at work. It seems as though whatever happens at home has a sort of knock-on effect at work. If things are OK with the kids, then work goes fairly well. Otherwise . . . things would be so much better if I could settle down a bit. That doesn't seem likely unless my wife changes . . .

Let me just run over that with you again: If your wife were to settle down, things would improve at home and that would lead to your work being more productive?

Yes. It seems a bit unfair of me to say that 'my wife has got to change' but I know what I mean. It's sometimes a bit difficult to talk to her, that's all. I suppose she must find me pretty awkward . . . I know she thinks I'm a bit stubborn . . .

So, you seem to be saying that both of you are involved in the need to change . . . ?

Yes, exactly. We both need to sit down and sort things out.

In this extract, the counsellor remains, squarely, with what the client is saying, neither jumping in to offer an explanation of what might be going on nor offering advice about how the situation might be resolved but remaining instead with the concrete reality (ie with the picture that the client is offering of his situation).

It could be otherwise. Consider the following example. Here, the counsellor does not remain concrete and this, in turn, leads to other complications:

I don't know. I just seem to get things sorted out and then all sorts of things happen at work. It seems as though whatever happens at home has a sort of knock-on effect at work. If things are OK with the kids, then work goes fairly well. Otherwise . . . things would be so much better if I could settle down a bit. That doesn't seem likely unless my wife changes . . .

It sounds, to me, as though you expect an awful lot from your wife. Why does she have to change?

Well, it's not a simple as that, I suppose. But if she doesn't change, then things at work are likely to stay the same.

Yes, but is it fair to blame your wife?

I'm not blaming her. I just feel she has to change a bit. With all due respect, you don't really know the situation at home ... it's difficult to explain. I'm sorry I brought it up, really.

No. Its important that you did bring it up. It's only when we get to the bottom of what is happening at home that we can begin to sort out the work situation ... it seems to me.

It is easy to play the amateur (or even professional) psychologist but it is rarely productive. The point is to stay with what the client has to say and to explore it. Any interpretation by the counsellor and any too easily offered advice is unlikely to be particularly helpful. In a way, the concept of concreteness brings together almost all of the essential elements of the counselling process. The counsellor who remains concrete is more likely to listen to, accept and not judge the client, and is less likely to jump in with 'quick fix' solutions or advice. In the end, the best counselling is a fairly silent affair on the part of the counsellor. It is the client who should do most of the talking.

A sense of humour

A sense of humour can rescue most situations. That is not to say that the effective counsellor becomes some sort of stand-up comedian, nor takes lightly what the client has to say. Gentle use of humour can help the client to regain sight of the 'larger canvas'. People who have problems often become narrow in their focus. They ponder on their own situation and it takes priority over almost everything else. It is easy, for all of us, to blow things out of proportion. The counsellor who has a 'light' approach can often ease tension and help the client towards a greater sense of perspective. Indeed, this may be just what the comedian does: takes sensitive and even taboo subjects and makes light of them. We laugh both from relief and from a realization that 'big' topics are not necessarily 'sacred' ones. So it can be in counselling.

A sense of the tragic

Almost paradoxically, alongside a sense of humour goes a sense of the tragic. No one can get very involved with another person's problems without also developing what the Spanish philosopher, Miquel de Unamuno (1954) called the 'tragic sense of life'. We are human and we have human limitations. We create, for ourselves, dramas of sometimes epic proportions. We are often unable to sort those dramas out. A sense of this tragic side of being human can help the counsellor both to retain his or her own humanity and to remain humble. Counsellors are not people who have more answers than other people – they are usually just people who will listen more readily than some others.

Self-awareness

Linked to the tragic sense of life is the need for counsellors to become self-aware. This is to say that they should know something of their own problems and limitations – and also their strengths. Self-awareness, in this sense, is not some navel-gazing searching for an 'inner self' but a practical attempt at identifying how we compare with and come across to other people. If we are to set ourselves up as people who can, in a minimal way, help other people, it seems reasonable to ask that we also explore our own life situations. Part of all counselling-skills workshops and courses should be dedicated to such self-exploration to a practical end. The final chapter of this book offers some simple activities for developing self-awareness.

STAGES IN THE COUNSELLING PROCESS

Sometimes counselling is a prolonged affair and sometimes people can be helped in a relatively short space of time. When a counselling relationship develops, it is not uncommon to see certain stages being worked through. These may be identified as follows:

1. Getting started.
2. Introductory talk.
3. Identifying the issues.
4. Coping with feelings.
5. Identifying possible solutions.
6. Agreeing a plan.
7. Implementing the plan.

This list of stages can be useful in thinking about how to structure the counselling process.

Getting started

Here, the counsellor and client meet and get to know each other. Often, the client will be nervous and will not know what to say. In this stage of the relationship, it is usually helpful if the counsellor plays the dominant role and helps the client to relax, settle down and focus on why they are there. This is as true in careers counselling as it is in counselling for emotional problems. Few people are able to 'come right out with it' in the early stages of the relationship. In this stage, it is useful if the counsellor clarifies the following issues with the client:

- the frequency with which they will meet;
- the times they will meet;
- when it is anticipated that the relationship will end;
- whether or not the two can talk confidentially.

Also, it is helpful if the counsellor indicates that *anything* can be talked about. This creates the opportunity for the client to talk about what he or she wants to talk about.

Introductory talk

Most people come to a counsellor with only a vague sense of what it is they really want to talk about. Many start from a general conversation about their lives and then work towards specifics. It seems likely that many people do not know what is troubling them until they begin to talk. This stage of the relationship, then, is a general, opening stage in which the client is encouraged to give the counsellor a few personal details. Here, it is useful to use broad, open questions such as:

- Can you tell me something about your work at the present time?
- Can you tell me a little about your background?
- How have you found the course so far?
- What have you been doing with the company up to now?

These allow the client to get talking and often prove the point that: 'I don't know what I think and feel until I hear what I say.'

Identifying the issues

At a point during this initial phase of talking, the 'real' issues begin to emerge. Sometimes, such issues can be brought to the surface by the counsellor asking 'facilitative' questions that encourage the client to elaborate a little. Examples of such interventions include:

- How did you feel about that?
- What was that like?
- How are you feeling at the moment?
- What did you do then?
- What happened when you did that?

This sort of question encourages the client to say more and helps to focus on the 'real' issues. One important principle emerges out of this discussion. It is important to note that the things that are 'real issues' for the client, may not be 'real issues' for the counsellor and vice versa. (The things that worry me may not worry you.) What is really important in all types of counselling is that the counsellor does not anticipate or 'best guess' what the important issues are for the client. In all cases, those issues should emerge out of, and be identified by, the client's discussion of his or her own life situation. Consider what can happen when this is not the case:

My father died and I moved away from the area. I found it difficult to settle down and went from job to job. I never found it easy to settle on the right job.

I know what that's like. It took me a long time to settle after my father died. I suppose we need to face all sorts of feelings when someone close to us dies . . .

No, it wasn't really like that. I was never particularly close to my father . . . What was really difficult was that I didn't have any formal qualifications. I only really settled after I got myself to university.

Hopefully, the point is clear. It is easy to be wrong when anticipating what another person's problems might be.

Coping with feelings

Counselling people often means coping with emotions. Once people in counselling begin to identify the real issues, they often begin to experience emotional release. A considerable part of the process of helping people in counselling is concerned with the emotional or 'feelings' side of the person. In the UK and North American cultures, a great premium is placed on the individual being able to 'control' feelings, and thus overt expression of emotion is often frowned upon. As a result, we learn to bottle up feelings, sometimes from a very early age. In this chapter, we will consider the effects of such suppression of emotion and identify some practical ways of helping people to identify and explore their feelings.

Before going further, a word of caution. It is often noted that people are individual in their responses. It is difficult to make general statements about 'how human beings work'. If we *do* make generalizations, we are likely to find exceptions to them. It should be noted, then, that while the points made in this chapter are true of many people, they are not necessarily true of *all* people. Some people, for example, do not particularly like or want to express strong feelings. There is no need to have an elaborate theory of 'resistance' or denial here but merely to note that different people do things differently. There should be no hint from the counsellor that people *should* release or face emotions. It is important to pay close attention to the individual's needs and wants. We are all different and *vive la différence!*

Feelings

It is possible to distinguish between at least four types of emotion that are commonly suppressed or bottled up: anger, fear, grief and embarrassment. It is suggested that there is a relationship between these feelings and certain expressions of them. Thus, in counselling, anger may be expressed as loud sound, fear as trembling, grief through tears and embarrassment by laughter. It is suggested, too, that there is a relationship between those feelings and certain basic human needs.

We all have the need to understand and know what is happening to us. If that knowledge is not forthcoming, we may experience fear. We need, also, to make choices in our lives and if that choice is restricted in certain ways we may feel anger. Thirdly, we need to experience the expression of love and of being loved. If that love is denied or taken away from us, we may experience grief. To these basic human needs may be added the need for self-respect and dignity. If such dignity is denied us, we may feel self-conscious and embarrassed.

Mostly, people can be helped if their emotions are accepted by the counsellor. If a person begins to cry, for example, it is usually better if they are allowed to do so and if no attempt is made to stop them prematurely. The table opposite identifies some of the ways in which the counsellor can help with feelings in the counselling role. The first column illustrates some typical client presentations to the counsellor. The second column suggests interventions that the counsellor might make to help the client. What is notable about this cycle of events is that the expression of emotion seems to be both a natural and a curative factor. Often the client, once having expressed emotion, feels better able to identify a desirable course of action. Things seem a bit clearer after emotional expression.

Identifying possible solutions

Once feelings have been relieved, the next stage involves helping the client to identify ways to deal with or cope with the problem(s). Not everything can be sorted out. Not everything has a solution. The point, here, is that the client has now identified a situation that was unclear or, perhaps, unbearable before. The next thing is to work out a plan to make the situation more liveable. Most counselling theorists agree that it is the *client* who should identify solutions to problems. This process can be encouraged by a 'brainstorming' session.

In brainstorming, the client is encouraged to think diversely about possible ways of resolving his or her present situation. Nothing need be excluded at this stage. The client is encouraged to be creative, irrational and spontaneous as well as thoughtful, logical and sensible. The idea is to generate as many solutions as possible. Out of this usually comes an 'obvious' solution. Obvious, that is, to the client. Often, this stage of counselling involves what has been called an 'ah-ha!' experience. Suddenly, but often inevitably, the solution to the problem under discussion dawns on the client.

Client Status	Counsellor Role
1. The client feels 'blocked' and unable to move on in the counselling relationship; acknowledges inability to express feelings.	1. The counsellor listens and accepts and does not offer advice or prescription, rather, helping the client to focus on feelings.
2. The client begins to experience some of his or her feelings. Conversation changes very specifically from 'I sometimes get very upset' to 'I am very upset'.	2. The counsellor listens and encourages the expression of emotion.
3. The client may experience catharsis: the expression of tears, anger, fear or laughter.	3. The counsellor is supportive and allows full expression.
4. The client sits and reflects quietly, following the cathartic release. This may be a lengthy process.	4. No interventions are necessary. The client is working through a natural process. The counsellor remains supportive and quiet.
5. The client feels refreshed and more able to move on to identifying priorities and to problem-solving.	5. The counsellor takes cues from the client and allows the relationship to move on at the client's pace.

Agreeing a plan

Out of the process of reaching an idea about how things might be resolved comes the need to identify a practical plan of action. It is one thing knowing what you want to do or change; it is another thing to put those ideas into action. During this stage of the counselling relationship, both counsellor and client work together to draw up a practical plan of action. For some, it is helpful if this plan is committed to paper. Other people prefer a more relaxed approach to such planning. The point is that the plan should be both reasonable and achievable.

Implementing the plan

This stage of counselling is carried out by the client almost independently of the counsellor. It is the putting into action of the plan that was discussed in the previous stage. Usually, what the client needs here is support from the counsellor. Change is difficult for most people: it often brings with it a degree of anxiety and it is the counsellor's function to help the client to deal with that anxiety. Often, too, this stage of the relationship heralds its end, and both client and counsellor have to deal with the fact that they might not be meeting for much longer. It is tempting to think that this is only a problem for the client. In practice, counsellors usually get attached to the people they counsel. It is necessary, then, for both parties to think about – and if necessary talk about – the closing of the relationship. Once it is decided that it *will* end, it is often best to set a date and to make the break a clean one. One of the manoeuvres that counsellors who are attached to their clients sometimes use, almost unconsciously, is to put off the final counselling session. Alternatively, they suggest that 'one more meeting' might be useful. The clean break seems to be the best approach for both client and counsellor.

These, then, are the stages that many counselling relationships work through. Not all relationships follow the stages in this order and sometimes one stage or more is left out. The framework offered here is a way of *thinking* about the counselling process and can help to give some structure to the relationship. This is particularly useful in the early stages of counselling courses and workshops. The next consideration is that of counselling skills.

COUNSELLING SKILLS

The literature on the theory of counselling is vast and the reader is referred to some of it for a more detailed discussion of counselling philosophy and psychology (Rogers 1967, Nelson-Jones 1984, Heron 1990, Burnard 1989, Egan 1990). Drawing from that literature, it is possible to identify the following categories of counselling skills:

- listening;
- giving information;
- making suggestions;
- drawing out;
- challenging;
- supporting.

Listening

Listening is the most important skill in counselling. It is the process of 'hearing' the other person. This involves not only noting the things that they say but also a whole range of other aspects of communication. Given the wide range of ways in which one person tries to communicate with another, this is further evidence of the need to develop the ability to offer close and sustained attention, as outlined above.

Three aspects of listening can be identified here. Linguistic aspects of speech refer to the actual words that the client uses, to the phrases they choose and to the metaphors they use to convey how they are feeling. Attention to such metaphors is often useful as metaphorical language can often convey more than can more conventional use of language (Cox 1990). Paralinguistics refers to all those aspects of speech that are not words, themselves. Thus, timing, volume, pitch, accent are all paralinguistic aspects of communication. Paralinguistics can only offer us a possible clue to how the other person is feeling. It is important that we check with the client the degree to which that clue matches with the client's own perception of the way they feel.

Non-verbal aspects of communication refer to 'body language': expression through the use of the body. Thus facial expression, use of gestures, body position and movement, proximity to the counsellor, touch in relation to the counsellor, all offer further clues about the client's internal status beyond the words they use and can be 'listened' to by the attentive counsellor. Again, any assumptions that we make about what such body language 'means' need to be clarified with the client. There is a temptation to believe that body language can be 'read', as if we all used it in the same sort of way. Reflection on the subject, however, will reveal that body language is dependent to a large degree on a wide number of variables: the context in which it occurs, the nature of the relationship, the individual's personal style and preference, the personality of the person 'using' the body language, and so on. It is once again safer, therefore, not to assume that we 'know' what another person is 'saying' with their body language but to treat it as a clue and to clarify its meaning with the client. Thus it is preferable, in counselling, merely to bring to the client's attention the way they are sitting, or their facial expression, rather than to offer an interpretation of it. Two examples may help here. In the first, the counsellor is offering an interpretation and an assumption:

> *I notice from the way that you have your arms folded and from your frown that you are uncomfortable with discussing things at home.*

In the second example, the counsellor merely feeds back such observations to the client and allows the *client* to clarify the situation:

> *I notice that you have your arms folded and that you're frowning. What are you feeling at the moment?*

Giving information

How much information is given during a counselling session will depend on the nature of the counselling relationship. It is fairly safe to say that it is more possible to give information about concrete issues than it is about personal issues. Here are examples of those two categories:

Concrete issues
- expanding a business;
- developing a career;

- completing a college course;
- buying a house.

Personal issues
- continuing a relationship;
- coping with the death of a relative;
- developing self-awareness;
- working through depression.

In the first category, the expert counsellor will have access to particular and accurate information which can, when it is appropriate and when it is requested, be passed on to the client. In the second category, the client is the only 'expert'. The counsellor is rarely advised to try to offer 'information' in this field. It is sometimes easy to assume that because *we* have experienced certain life events (bereavement, the breaking up of a relationship and so forth), we will be able to share that experience with others in order to help them. While self-disclosure on the part of the counsellor is sometimes of value, simply to assume that the client's situation closely mimics ours is usually fraught. We all live in different 'lifeworlds': we all experience things differently. We cannot make assumptions about how other people live their lives nor about how they feel about different life events.

The personal construct psychologist, George Kelly (1969) summed up the safest position on this issue, as 'If you want to know what someone is about, ask them – they might just tell you.' The point is clear. The counsellor should not continually compare his or her life experience with that of the client, nor be too ready to share personal experience with the client in a benign, but ineffective, attempt at helping.

Making suggestions

Most of us slip easily into giving other people advice. Advice is a little like information except that it is not based on evidence of fact: it involves value judgements. Like information, suggestions are best kept for use in the 'concrete' domain. It is rarely useful in counselling to offer suggestions as to how the client may 'put his or her life right'. Just as it is important to hold back on information in counselling, so, too, is it vital that the counsellor does not too readily offer advice.

The problems with advice-giving are many and include the following pitfalls:

- people rarely take advice unless they feel that it is the 'right' advice, in which case they will usually have thought of it themselves;
- some people can become dependent on the advice of others. To begin to accept other people's advice is a seductive process. Once another person does the thinking for you, it is easy to become dependent;
- people may not like you for offering advice that does not turn out right;
- every time you offer people advice you rob them of the chance to figure things out for themselves – in other words, advice-giving can inhibit learning.

Drawing out

Some of the most useful counselling interventions are those that involve helping the client to verbalize what he or she is thinking and feeling. If counselling is a form of 'talking cure', then letting the client speak is one of the most important aspects of it. Various activities in the second part of this book deal with this aspect of counselling. Examples of the sort of counselling interventions that help to draw out the client include:

- *Open questions*. These are the sort that do not have one correct answer nor do they usually have a one-word answer. An example of an open question is: 'How did you feel when that happened?'
- *Closed questions*. These are questions that usually produce a yes or no answer. They are not as useful as open questions for drawing out but they can help to clarify particular issues. An example of such a question is: 'Have you talked this through with your wife?'
- *Reflection*. Reflection is the echoing back of the last few words that the client has spoken. It is a type of intervention that is widely used in 'Rogerian' counselling (Rogers 1952, 1967). An example of its use follows:

We moved to London at the end of the seventies but none of us

*really settled down. My wife never did like living in the city.
I found it difficult to get a job . . .*

You found it difficult to get a job . . .

*Well, it was difficult to start with, anyway. I suppose I didn't
really want to get one, if the truth be told . . .*

You didn't want one . . .

Reflection, used skilfully, can be a great aid to helping another
person to clarify his thoughts and feelings. Used clumsily, it can
make the conversation sound like a travesty of the counselling
process. It is recommended that all trainees in counselling-skills
workshops get plenty of practice in using the intervention so that it
becomes 'second nature' to them. Reflection is easily spotted if it is
used by someone who is not comfortable with the intervention. In
the end, you need to get so good at using it that you no longer even
notice that you use it.

Challenging

Sometimes it is helpful to challenge what the client is saying.
Although challenging and confronting are not always associated
with counselling, there are times when they are appropriate. For
example:

- When the client states something that is clearly not the case (eg
  'There is no one in this organization that I can talk to at all').
- When the client continues to self-denigrate (eg 'I've never been
  any good at anything. I've always been a failure, right from the
  word go').
- When the client appears to be avoiding certain issues (eg
  'There's nothing wrong . . . nothing at all . . . I wonder why I am
  sitting here talking to you really').

Challenging, in counselling, must also be supportive. The point of
this sort of confrontation is never to show up or tell off the client. It
is to help the client move on a little, to encourage them to examine
other aspects of the problem. Like advice-giving, it is an intervention
that should be used very cautiously and with great tact. It should
not be used as a veiled form of disciplinary hearing nor should it be

rationalized by the counsellor as 'plain speaking'. Challenging should always be an intentional act and used with great care.

Supporting

The whole of the counselling process should be an act of support. The counsellor, for much of the time, is the client's advocate. He or she should aim at befriending the client. Thus, all counselling interventions that are made should be made in a spirit of encouragement and care. The aim of counselling is never to moralize or 'put things right'. It is to help the client find his or her own way through a series of life problems which *the client* has identified. The counsellor is, as it were, a 'fellow traveller' and not a person who is somehow better equipped for life than the client. In this sense, too, the counsellor should retain humility. However long a person practises counselling, it never makes him or her a 'better' person. He or she is just as human and just as fallible as every client.

PITFALLS AND PROBLEMS AND HOW TO OVERCOME THEM

Dependence

Dependence is a double-edged problem. On the one hand, most of us like the idea that other people need us. On the other, most of us also appreciate that other people need to think and act independently. The fact that counselling occurs at all suggests that people who work in a counselling capacity are prepared, to at least a minimal degree, to take some responsibility for part of another person's life. Even if they only listen to the other person, they are still accepting the responsibility of responding to what that person is saying.

Any sort of personal disclosure is likely to bring with it a degree of dependence. Think, if you can, of something that you have never told *anyone*. Now consider what sort of relationship you would have with the person that you *did* tell about that issue. Think, also, how that relationship might develop if you often discussed the issue with that person. It seems reasonable to suppose that you might become dependent on him or her. The fact that another person agrees to listen to intimate and often painful things not only makes you grateful but also encourages you to lean on that person and to look to them for support. It is this pattern that is often repeated in counselling relationships.

How can dependence be coped with? First, it is not always such a burden. As we have noted, it is often pleasant and manageable to have another person look to you for help. One of the best ways of keeping some sort of balance in the relationship is to take some time, every so often, to discuss the relationship itself. That is to say that both counsellor and client occasionally step out of the counselling relationship and talk about how they are getting on with each other. This process of review and discussion can often help to maintain the fragile balance between slight and total dependence. Second, the time-frame can affect the degree of dependence. If the client and counsellor meet at preset times and for a specific length of time, then the dependence issue can usually be managed quite well. Over-dependence often develops when the counsellor does not know how to structure time. In this case, the client is allowed unlimited access. This may mean that the client has the counsellor's home number and licence to 'ring at any time'. It is suggested that scheduling the counselling meetings more carefully can help both client and counsellor to keep a usefully therapeutic distance. It does not always work of course, but if both client and counsellor stay aware of developing dependence, then the issue can usually be worked on. It is when dependence develops without either party being aware of it that the problems start. Anyone starting out in counselling would do well to think through the question of dependence carefully.

The language problem

All professional groups develop their own language. Sometimes jargon is a useful 'shorthand' for conveying complicated ideas in a straightforward way. Counselling and interpersonal-skills training has also developed its own language style. In a recent study (Burnard 1991) of interpersonal-skills trainers I noted two particular styles. The first I call the 'alternative' style because it mimics the type of language used in the 'alternative' press of the 1960s and the hippy slang of that period. People who adopt the alternative style tend to say things like, 'Can I share something with you?' or 'I want to find out a little more about where you are coming from'.

The other style, I called 'existentialese'. In this language style, people talk about concepts that are frequently discussed by existentialist philosophers but do not usually convey a clear sense of meaning. Examples, drawn from my study, include, 'We need to experience and encounter the concrete sense of self,' and 'To say "you" to a person is to validate that person, to accept them and to fully appreciate them.'

It is difficult to know exactly what people who speak and write like this really mean. It is suggested, therefore, that both styles of language are best avoided. Given that one of the main aims of counselling is to communicate with and understand another person, it is important that when we speak we are clear about what it is we are trying to express. Using this sort of jargon does not help. The way to avoid using language styles of this sort is to monitor yourself constantly. We all need to pay attention to what we say and how we say it. It is even more important that we do so if we set out to counsel other people.

Burnout

The term 'burnout' is usually used to describe the feelings associated with long-term, job-related stress. Counsellors are particularly prone to it because they work so closely with other people. Maslach (1981) suggests that:

> Burnout is a syndrome of emotional exhaustion, depersonalization, and reduced personal accomplishment that can occur among individuals who do 'people work' of some kind. It is a response to the chronic emotional strain of dealing extensively with other human beings, particularly when they are troubled or having problems. Thus, it can be considered one type of job stress.

Burnout is usually associated with working in caring professions, under considerable stress, for long periods. Characteristics include:

* loss of motivation;
* the development of negative rather than positive attitudes towards the job and towards other people;
* the development of a 'gallows' sense of humour or a loss of sense of humour altogether;

- a sense of a narrowing choice of options;
- a feeling that one is acted upon rather than exercising choice.

Maslach identifies three stages in the process of burnout: emotional exhaustion, depersonalization and feelings of reduced personal accomplishment.

Emotional exhaustion
The first characteristic of the onset of burnout is a sense of emotional fatigue. The counsellor feels that he or she has little left to give to others and begins to cope with this by gradually shutting off from others. This leads to stage two – depersonalization.

Depersonalization
In this stage, the fact of cutting oneself off from others as a coping strategy leads to a sense of alienation. Others are also viewed in a negative light and the professional often actively begins to dislike those people previously cared for or worked with. It is not uncommon to hear professionals remark in a cynical way 'this job would be OK if it weren't for the clients' – for the person experiencing burnout, this sentiment becomes a reality. Often the person expends a lot of energy in trying to avoid clients and other people – sometimes by burying himself or herself in paperwork and administration, sometimes by keeping appointments very brief. Overall, the feeling is one of negative attitudes towards self and others.

Reduced personal accomplishment
All this distancing takes its toll. The person experiencing burnout ends up by feeling that they are achieving very little. In some cases this is true. In others, the negative attitude leads to an inability to self-assess or to evaluate work outcomes. Sometimes, all past work is 'rubbished'. The burntout person comes to feel that *nothing* she or he has done in the field of caring has been worthwhile and that any previously held view of themselves as 'caring' was delusory. It is at this point that many people choose to leave the profession altogether and seek work in a situation where they can avoid other people. Others learn to cope by adopting a distant or cynical approach.

Coping with burnout

Pines, Aronson and Kafry (1981) suggest four major strategies for coping with burnout:

- being aware of the problem;
- taking responsibility for doing something about it;
- achieving some degree of cognitive clarity;
- developing new tools for coping.

Being aware of the problem
The first stage must be recognizing that a problem exists at all. This is not always easy as the process of burnout is often insidious. Sometimes the change of attitude in the person experiencing burnout is noted by a colleague and this offers the chance for discussion of the problem. Even then, it is common for the burntout person to deny that anything is wrong or, if there is, to see the problem as being external to themselves. Very often, that person's distress is displaced on to the job, the organization or on to other people. Thus it is not uncommon to hear people suffering from this type of stress reaction to claim that the organization 'no longer cares' for them, or that 'the job has changed and isn't interesting any more'. Rarely can the person 'own' the problem and identify that, while the job and the clients have contributed to burnout, the problem lies within. This recognition must occur if something is to change.

Taking responsibility for doing something about it
Linked to identifying that a problem exists is the recognition that, if anything is to change, the person with burnout must take the initiative in doing something about it. Unfortunately, this is usually what they feel least able to do. They often feel powerless and demotivated to the point of merely being able to struggle through. This is where help from colleagues and friends can make the difference. By talking through the issues and being heard by another person, the counsellor with burnout can come to the decision to change his or her situation.

Achieving cognitive clarity
Burnout has a distinct emotional component. As we have noted, the burntout person often feels trapped and disinterested. The point, in this stage, is to itemize carefully exactly what the issues are that are

contributing to the state of burnout. It is never only the case that a person feels emotionally exhausted. Things are happening to them that *make* them feel that way. Careful analysis of what is happening in the person's life and work can lead to the identification of solutions.

Developing new skills for coping

The process of gaining cognitive clarity leads to the development of ways of coping with burnout. Nothing else changes unless a behavioural change occurs. The first stage in achieving such behavioural change is the identification of clear objectives, as noted above. This is not to suggest that *everything* that contributes to a person feeling burntout can be changed, but certainly with clear goals *some* things can be changed. The point about such goals is that they need to be clearly stated and achievable.

Things getting out of control

It is a common fear among people new to counselling that 'things might get out of control'. This can often be translated to mean one or more of the following:

- the client may begin to cry or become hysterical;
- the client may become mentally ill;
- the client may begin to talk about very complicated issues that you are not capable of dealing with.

It may be useful to consider each of these in turn.

Crying and hysteria

As we have noted, the expression of emotion is usually a therapeutic occurrence. Most people who have bottled up emotions tend to feel a certain release and even a gain in insight when they begin to let themselves cry. Also, contrary to popular belief, crying rarely gets 'out of control'. Emotional release is usually self-limiting and if the client is allowed to express feelings in a warm and supportive atmosphere, they will usually find their own level and get to a point where they stop crying. There is certainly no recorded instance of a person failing to stop crying!

The term 'hysteria' is a little misleading. Sometimes, people who are new to the mental-health field or to counselling, imagine that if people are allowed to express themselves fully, then they may become uncontrollably upset. Again, it is difficult to find instances of this in the literature or in the research into counselling and psychotherapy. It would seem that this is more of an anxious fantasy than a reality.

Mental illness
People do not 'become' mentally ill by talking about their problems. Some people, may, of course, be mentally ill before they start talking but it seems likely, in the sort of contexts that we have discussed so far, that the counsellor is likely to know of this before counselling begins. In cases where this is not known and in which the client begins to express ideas that indicate mental illness, it is best to refer the person to other agencies for help. In the first instance, this will normally be the person's general practitioner.

Complicated issues
Many life situations are complicated. The fact that we are human means that we tend to get ourselves caught up in difficult personal and emotional situations. It does not follow, though, that the counsellor is required to 'sort out' all these difficulties. As we have noted, counselling cannot be a panacea for all life's difficulties. Almost everyone, though, benefits from being able to talk about even the most complicated problems. Usually, the process of being allowed to talk things through makes a difference. Often, we are frightened by what *we* might feel if we have to listen to very difficult life circumstances. Sometimes, in counselling, it is simply a question of exercising a certain bravery and a definite altruism. We have, as it were, to forget ourselves and give our attention fully to the other person. After all, the problems under discussion belong to the other person. They are not our problems – however much we may associate ourselves with them. This maintenance of 'ego boundaries' is an essential part of the counselling process. It is vital that we always remember the difference between the client and ourselves and between our problems and theirs. This is not to suggest that we become hard-hearted or thick-skinned but merely to note that we can be of great help if we allow another person full expression – even if we don't like what we hear.

Counselling checklist

1. Are you clear about the way *you* use the term *'counselling'*?

2. What do *you* feel are the important personal qualities needed to be an effective counsellor?

3. What particular counselling skills do you use most frequently?

Chapter 2:

Managing counselling-skills training

AIMS OF THE CHAPTER

This chapter focuses on:

- planning counselling-skills training;
- planning workshops;
- running workshops.

PLANNING COUNSELLING-SKILLS TRAINING

The training of counsellors poses something of a problem. Counselling is a very human activity involving a great many variables, contexts, people, times and situations. To generalize about what 'good' counselling training involves is difficult. In the paragraphs below are some of the various issues that need to be addressed by anyone working in the field. This list is not exhaustive but it does both help to highlight the complexity of the task and offer a framework for addressing that complexity.

Theory issues

First, what sort of counselling are you training people in? As was noted in the previous chapter, there are various ways of defining counselling. There are also a good many theoretical positions that have been adopted in relation to it. While it is probably true to say that the client-centred approach to counselling has dominated the field for the last 20 or so years, that is changing. Today, it is possible to identify at least the following approaches to counselling:

- *The humanistic approach.* Within this approach is subsumed the client-centred method advocated by Carl Rogers (1952, 1967) and also other theories of the human condition including gestalt therapy (Perls 1969), six-category intervention analysis (Heron 1990) and existential counselling (Van Durzen Smith 1989).
- *The psychodynamic approach.* Counsellors who work in this approach generally draw from the psychoanalytical theory outlined by Freud and his followers (Hall 1954). A more recent development of psychodynamic thinking is to be found in Berne's transactional analysis (Berne 1972).
- *The behavioural approach.* This pragmatic orientation towards counselling focuses on identifying behaviour patterns that are no longer effective or required and developing programmes for changing those behaviours. Theoretically, it is diametrically opposed to the psychodynamic approach.
- *The cognitive approach.* Counsellors in this field acknowledge that how we think about ourselves influences not only what we do but also what we feel. In this approach to counselling, clients' illogical and irrational thoughts are challenged by the counsellor.

From the point of view of counselling training, it seems vital that any trainer first be acquainted with the theory underlying the particular sort of counselling they are advocating. While eclecticism is possible (and, in the end, most counsellors probably are eclectic), in the early stages of training a sound theoretical justification for what is being proposed in a training workshop is vital.

Personal issues

What are your reasons for running counselling skills workshops or courses? Are you simply responding to a demand or are you also trying to change the situation in which you work? Personal values, beliefs and attitudes need to be considered before counselling training is started. In some areas of the field there is a certain 'evangelism' for particular approaches to counselling. It seems important that everyone who is engaged in the process of trying to change the behaviour of others is clear about their motives for doing so.

Self-awareness

Linked to the personal issues identified above is the issue of self-awareness. Such awareness is never complete; we can never say that we have finished becoming self-aware. We can, however, explore our own problems and the ways we face or avoid them. We can also identify our own behavioural patterns in various life situations. This is not to say that all prospective counselling trainers have to engage in personal therapy but to acknowledge the need for everyone in the field to remain open to their own faults, strengths, biases and values. If we do not make these overt, at least to ourselves, we run the risk of passing them on to others without realizing it. Better, perhaps, to engage at least minimally in some self-analysis.

Interpersonal issues

Reflection on self is not enough. Trainers must also examine their relationships with others. All counselling trainers are role models for the style of counselling that they are advocating, therefore it seems reasonable that trainers will develop an increasing awareness of the effect that they have on others. There is no place in counselling-skills training for dogma or certainty. The whole field is constantly in a state of flux. We must remain humble about the amount we know about the human condition and this humility can develop out of a day to day study of how we get on with colleagues, friends and family.

Contextual issues

Counselling takes place in a range of settings. The sort of counselling that takes place in health care settings may or may not be appropriate in the business and management field. There is a danger in assuming that skills necessarily transfer directly from one field to another, although sometimes, of course, they do. There is a case here for exploring the field in which counselling will take place, before starting counselling-skills training. Listening to senior staff, consultants, managers, directors and so forth will help to 'place' the style of counselling training that is being sought. There is rarely a place for an 'off the shelf' approach to setting up counselling-skills training. Usually, training schemes need to be shaped to suit the organization.

Political issues

Counselling is not an apolitical act; for some, it is very conservative. This is particularly true of the client-centred variety in which little attempt is made to address the wider context of people's problems. In the client-centred approach, the answers to problems in a person's life always lie within themselves. The danger, here, is that nothing gets changed within the rest of that person's life-world. Clearly, many problems derive from the circumstances in which people live and work. To ask only the individual to change may seem, to some people, a naive approach to dealing with problems and they may want to take a broader approach to dealing with problems and problem situations.

Also, when we counsel, whatever our theoretical position, we are offering the client a particular set of values. If for example, we adopt the client-centred approach, we are offering, too, the view that individuals *can* change their personal lives. If we offer a psychodynamic approach, we are also offering the view that early childhood experiences have contributed to the present situation. All these values need to be examined during counselling training as well as during the counselling practice that follows from such training. Masson (1990) dismisses all counselling and psychotherapy as inappropriate activities to engage in because of just this point. He maintains that all counselling and therapy involve the imposition of one set of values (the counsellor's) on another person (the client). This point of view is always an interesting one to explore in counselling skills courses and workshops.

PLANNING WORKSHOPS

Chapters 4 and 5 offer detailed checklists for use when planning the content of counselling skills workshops. Before those chapters, it is important to anticipate some of the considerations that need to be made by anyone who plans to set up workshops.

What type of workshop?

First of all, what type of workshop is going to be organized? Workshops can vary in a number of dimensions:

- who will attend?
- how long will the workshop run?
- where will the workshop be run?
- what are the aims of the workshop?

Who will attend?
Who is the workshop for? There are important differences between running a workshop for those who choose to attend for whatever reason and those who are 'sent'. The former types of workshop are usually easier to organize and run as everyone is highly motivated. On the other hand, people in this category may be more critical of what is offered in your workshop. You need to make sure that everyone is clear about the aims and scope of the workshop.

If courses are run in house, there may be problems with people being forced to attend. If this is the case, the issue needs to be addressed early on in the life of the workshop. Sometimes it is necessary to allow for a considerable period of time in which trainees' attitudes towards the workshop are discussed. If this is necessary, it is best if the trainer avoids defensiveness but meets all criticism and objections in a level and open way. A case, perhaps, of the soft answer turning away wrath.

How long will the workshop run?
Workshops can be anything from one day to two weeks in length. Others run over a series of weekends and longer courses can be planned. If one- or two-year courses are organized, it is often a good idea to link up with a local college or university department in order that the course is certificated. Most people who are prepared to invest a considerable amount of time into this sort of venture will appreciate something concrete to show for their efforts. Also, many firms will only release and finance their employees if the course does offer a certificate or diploma. Negotiations with colleges and universities take time and usually a detailed protocol is required

along with very particular details of assessment and evaluation procedures.

Where will the workshop be run?
All the activities in this book depend on trainees being able to make use of some space. Many of the exercises involve people pairing off to practise elements of the counselling process. As this is the case, it is important that the workshop is run in a room (or a series of rooms) large enough for this to happen. If space is a problem, it is often better to keep workshop numbers low, although this may put up the overall cost. A balance needs to be kept between pricing the workshop competitively and making sure that all your costs as facilitator and organizer are met.

What are the aims of the workshop?
What do you want people to achieve from attending your workshop? You may, on the one hand want to predetermine the outcomes of your workshop fairly precisely and to state those outcomes as behavioural objectives. Increasingly, and in line with adult-learning theory (Jarvis 1986, Knowles 1990), there is a tendency to negotiate the aims of workshops and similar learning experiences with the participants. There remains one problem. If you do not declare your aims at all, you run the risk of no one knowing what your workshop will be about. It is often a good idea to compromise a little and to declare broad aims such as the following:

The workshop will enable participants to:

- *identify their own learning needs in the field of counselling;*
- *explore a range of counselling skills;*
- *discuss the application of those skills to their own area of practice.*

However such aims are stated, it is important that the counselling skills that are practised in your workshop can be transferred back to the 'real' situation – the place in which trainees work. Transfer of learning, in the field of interpersonal skills, is one of the most difficult aspects of the process. It is not sufficient merely to show people a range of skills: it is vital that they can also apply them. If this does not happen, then the workshop will just appear as an interesting 'island' in the middle of their work and everyday experience. The point is for people to be able to apply what they learn.

Advertising the workshop

How will people know about your workshop? The cheapest form of broad advertising is often via local free papers. Local newspapers also run advertisements at reasonable rates and you may want to make full use of newsagents' and supermarkets' notice boards too.

If you prepare written material for advertising, make sure that your output is of professional quality. While many people have access to a computer, few have the necessary skills in desktop publishing required to make fliers, handouts and posters look really professional. Nor do poor-quality photocopies make much of an impression. Consider approaching two or three printers and asking them to quote you on a range of advertising materials.

The same can also be said of handouts that you use in the course of running your workshop. While you have permission to photocopy the relevant pages of this book for use in your course, make sure that other handouts are of high quality. In this case, computer-generated handouts will usually suffice – particularly if they are laser printed. Make sure, though, that you put very few words on each page. Use plenty of 'white space' and keep the whole thing simple. Do not use elaborate diagrams nor change type styles too often in the process of composing your work.

RUNNING WORKSHOPS

Once the workshop has been set up, and after participants have agreed to attend, all that is left to do is to contemplate how you will run it. Most workshops contain the following elements:

- a theory input;
- a description of counselling skills;
- practice of the skills through a variety of activities;
- evaluation of the workshop;
- application of the skills to the 'real' situation.

You may want to start the workshop with a series of lecturettes on the theory of counselling. Alternatively, you may prefer to generate the theory from an open discussion on counselling with trainees. Most people coming to counselling skills courses will have some ideas about what counselling is and what it is not. An initial discussion can do much to set the context and to clarify concepts. At some stage, however, it is important to make sure that counselling theory is formally identified. No workshop should be run solely on the basis of what is generated from discussion.

Before trainees take part in counselling skills activities, it is also important to identify the range of possible skills that they may want to use. One such framework was identified in the previous chapter. (The skills that were discussed there were listening, giving information, making suggestions, drawing out, challenging and supporting.)

John Heron offers an alternative analysis of counselling skills which he calls Six Category Intervention Analysis (Heron 1975). Heron's categories are:

- Informative interventions
- Prescriptive interventions
- Confronting interventions
- Cathartic interventions
- Catalytic interventions
- Supportive interventions

Heron calls the first three categories of intervention, (prescriptive, informative and confronting), 'authoritative' and suggests that in using these categories the practitioner retains control over the relationship. He calls the second three categories of intervention (cathartic, catalytic and supportive), 'facilitative' and suggests that these enable the client to retain control over the relationship. In other words, the first three are 'practitioner-centred' and the second three are 'client-centred'. (Another way of describing the difference between the first and second sets of three categories is that the first three are 'You tell me' interventions and the second three are 'I tell you' interventions.)

What, then, is the value of such an analysis of therapeutic interventions? First, it identifies the *range* of possible interventions available to the client and counsellor. Very often, in day to day interactions with others, we stick to repetitive forms of conversation and response simply because we are not aware that other options are available to us. This analysis identifies an exhaustive range of types of human intervention. Second, by identifying the sorts of intervention we can use, we can act more precisely and with a greater sense of intention. The counsellor/client relationship thus becomes more particular and less haphazard: we know *what* we are saying and also *how* we are saying it. We have greater interpersonal choice. Third, the analysis offers an instrument for training. Once the categories have been identified, they can be used by students and others to identify their weaknesses and strengths across the interpersonal spectrum. Counsellors can, in this way, develop a wide and comprehensive range of interpersonal skills.

Starting the workshop

The first stage of any workshop is one in which people get to know each other and the trainer. At this point, some people like to use 'icebreakers' or short activities that help people to relax and to learn something about other people on the course. Some of these are described in Chapter 5 and descriptions of others are offered elsewhere (Burnard 1992).

Some trainers prefer a more formal approach to opening and simply identify, with the group, the aims of the day, week or course. They then invite participants to state their names and to say something about themselves. It is worth taking some time over this initial stage of the workshop or course. The success of the workshop is often dependent on the way in which initial meetings are handled.

Keeping it going

Theory inputs and activities should, as a general rule, be short and sweet. No one wants to sit through lengthy lectures; nor should activities drag on indefinitely. All the activities described in Part II take less than an hour to complete and this is usually about the longest that people want to be engaged in one activity. Organize plenty of breaks and allow lots of time for free discussion. As a rule, follow the group and not your own schedule.

Ending the workshop

Saying goodbye is nearly as important as initial introductions. There should be plenty of time at the end of your workshop for people to discuss how they will transfer what they have learnt 'back to the ranch'. Some people may want to keep in touch with others. Sometimes, fairly involved relationships develop out of counselling-skills workshops. On the other hand, these intentions to stay in touch often remain just that – intentions. There is frequently a rush at the end of a workshop to swap addresses and telephone numbers, yet experience and the literature both suggest that these contacts are rarely pursued. If further contact *is* wanted, however, it is often a good idea to set up a 'recall' day in which participants meet again to discuss how they have applied the learning from the workshop. This can be an excellent way of reinforcing any learning that has occurred and you may want to build this idea into your overall plan.

Managing checklist
1. In order to be confident in running counselling skills workshops, what do *you* need to focus on most of all?
2. What has been *left out* of this chapter that *you* would have included?
3. What are the most important aspects of facilitation when running counselling skills courses and workshops?

Chapter 3:

Evaluating counselling-skills workshops

AIMS OF THE CHAPTER

This chapter focuses on:

- self and peer evaluation;
- an evaluation questionnaire.

All workshops need to be evaluated. In order to make sure that future ones are as successful or more successful than the present ones, methods need to be used to gain feedback at the end of a workshop. Two methods are identified in this chapter: self and peer evaluation and the use of a formal evaluative questionnaire.

SELF AND PEER EVALUATION

Self and peer evaluation is one means of identifying both personal and peer strengths and deficits at the end of a workshop. The point needs to be made that what is being evaluated is the trainee – not the course or workshop. These data, however, can be important to the trainer when thinking about planning future workshops.

The first stage of the self and peer evaluation process involves each member of the group spending a little time alone identifying both the positive and negative factors of their own performance during the workshop. These are written down as short notes. In the second stage, each person in turn undergoes self and peer evaluation. First, each trainee offers his or her own evaluation of their performance to the group. Then, peer evaluation can be requested and any one of the following options chosen:

- positive and negative evaluative comments from the group;
- only positive comments;
- only negative comments.

It seems unlikely that many people would choose the last option but it is included for completeness. Most people, in practice, ask for both positive and negative comments. When this happens, group members should be invited to make their comments directly to the participant and to state *first* the negative comments and then the positive. It is important that each participant finishes the process with positive comments. Group members should also be encouraged to remain tactful and supportive in their feedback. The trainer may also join in the self and peer evaluation process and this is to be recommended.

The self and peer evaluation process takes time and it is suggested that a whole afternoon be set aside for this activity. If required, the trainer can take notes of what is said or alternatively participants can be invited to leave their written comments with the trainer at the end of the workshop. Self and peer evaluation offers a potent and practical way of completing a counselling-skills workshop and the data developed through it can be useful in planning further workshops.

AN EVALUATION QUESTIONNAIRE

Another, more formal, way of evaluating a workshop is through the distribution of a questionnaire. The following pages offer one such questionnaire that can be photocopied and used in a workshop without further permission being sought. The questionnaire can be scored by attributing a value to each of the answer boxes, as follows:

Strongly Agree	Agree	Don't Know	Disagree	Strongly Disagree	Leave Blank
5	4	3	2	1	

Frequencies of the occurrence of each response can then be calculated and a profile of group responses can be obtained. The findings from this analysis can then be used in any one or more of a number of ways:

- the findings can be fed back to trainees to give them an overall sense of the success of the workshop;
- the findings can be used by you to modify your future workshops;
- the findings can be sent to managers and other sponsors.

Evaluation checklist

1. How do you rate *yourself* as a counsellor?

2. What are the limitations of self and peer evaluation?

3. How else could you use the questionnaire illustrated in this chapter?

COUNSELLING-SKILLS WORKSHOP EVALUATION
QUESTIONNAIRE

Read through each of the statements and then tick a box. You may strongly agree, agree, disagree or strongly disagree with each statement. You may also indicate that you 'don't know' about a particular item. Work fairly quickly through the statements; do not miss any out.

1. On the whole, I have enjoyed the workshop.

Strongly Agree	Agree	Don't Know	Disagree	Strongly Disagree	Leave Blank

2. I have had a considerable amount of practice as a counsellor during the workshop.

Strongly Agree	Agree	Don't Know	Disagree	Strongly Disagree	Leave Blank

3. Given the chance, I would undertake another course in counselling.

Strongly Agree	Agree	Don't Know	Disagree	Strongly Disagree	Leave Blank

4. I feel I have improved as a listener.

Strongly Agree	Agree	Don't Know	Disagree	Strongly Disagree	Leave Blank

5. The workshop was well organized.

Strongly Agree	Agree	Don't Know	Disagree	Strongly Disagree	Leave Blank

6. I will use what I have learned.

Strongly Agree	Agree	Don't Know	Disagree	Strongly Disagree	Leave Blank

7. I appreciated the work of the trainer in this workshop.

Strongly Agree	Agree	Don't Know	Disagree	Strongly Disagree	Leave Blank

8. Other people seemed to find the workshop useful.

Strongly Agree	Agree	Don't Know	Disagree	Strongly Disagree	Leave Blank

9. I would have liked more theory in the workshop.

Strongly Agree	Agree	Don't Know	Disagree	Strongly Disagree	Leave Blank

10. I would have liked more practice of the skills of counselling.

Strongly Agree	Agree	Don't Know	Disagree	Strongly Disagree	Leave Blank

11. Most people can benefit from counselling.

Strongly Agree	Agree	Don't Know	Disagree	Strongly Disagree	Leave Blank

12. Counselling should only be practised by trained professionals.

Strongly Agree	Agree	Don't Know	Disagree	Strongly Disagree	Leave Blank

13. I would do more counselling if I had the time.

Strongly Agree	Agree	Don't Know	Disagree	Strongly Disagree	Leave Blank

14. I intend to read more about counselling.

Strongly Agree	Agree	Don't Know	Disagree	Strongly Disagree	Leave Blank

15. I am better at confronting people than I was at the beginning of this workshop.

Strongly Agree	Agree	Don't Know	Disagree	Strongly Disagree	Leave Blank

16. Generally, I feel more confident as a result of this workshop.

Strongly Agree	Agree	Don't Know	Disagree	Strongly Disagree	Leave Blank

17. I would recommend this workshop to my colleagues.

Strongly Agree	Agree	Don't Know	Disagree	Strongly Disagree	Leave Blank

18. Real counselling skills come from real-life experience and not from counselling workshops.

Strongly Agree	Agree	Don't Know	Disagree	Strongly Disagree	Leave Blank

19. The workshop has improved my overall level of skill in counselling.

Strongly Agree	Agree	Don't Know	Disagree	Strongly Disagree	Leave Blank

Chapter 4:

Counselling-skills checklists

AIMS OF THE CHAPTER

This chapter offers a range of checklists on many aspects of counselling. The lists can be used in various ways. First, they can act as *aides mémoire*. Second, they can serve as the basis of handouts for counselling-skills workshops. Third, they can be turned into a series of points for discussion in a counselling-skills workshop. Also, they can help to stimulate further thinking about counselling. After all, no list of this sort is ever complete. It is important to try to identify the things that *you* would include on such lists.

CHARACTERISTICS OF A GOOD COUNSELLOR

- Personal warmth
- Genuineness
- Concreteness
- Unconditional positive regard
- Sense of humour
- Sense of the tragic

PSYCHOLOGICAL APPROACHES TO COUNSELLING

- *The client-centred approach.* This frequently used approach was developed by Carl Rogers (1952, 1967). It emphasizes the need for the counsellor to acknowledge that it is the counsellor who 'knows best' and de-emphasizes the giving of advice or the making of suggestions on the part of the counsellor.
- *The psychodynamic approach.* This is based on the work of Sigmund Freud and others (Hall 1954). Its central tenet is that we are all driven to a greater or lesser extent by our unconscious mind. The aim of psychodynamic counselling is to enable the client to make conscious some of the unconscious.
- *The gestalt approach.* The gestalt counsellor emphasizes the way in which we communicate with our bodies as well as verbally. It is an approach first developed by Fritz Perls (1969).
- *The humanistic approach.* The term 'humanistic' is an umbrella one for a range of often diverse types of counselling of which client-centred counselling is one. Humanistic psychology is sometimes referred to as the 'third force' in psychology after its rejection of both behavioural and psychodynamic approaches to the study of the person.
- *The personal construct approach.* George Kelly (1955) developed an idiosyncratic approach to discussing personal psychology. His theory of personal constructs and his concept of the 'person as scientist' have been developed as therapeutic tools.
- *The behavioural approach.* Behaviourism, an attempt to be scientific in psychology, inspired an approach to counselling which emphasizes the importance of studying behaviour, as it is only behaviour which is visible to other people when we communicate with them. The term 'behaviour', however, can be applied fairly broadly and some psychologists have it include verbal as well as non-verbal behaviour and also thinking ('cognitive behaviour').
- *The transactional analysis approach.* Transactional analysis, a neo-Freudian therapy, was developed by Eric Berne (1972). He argued that we meet the world from any one of three possible 'ego states': child, parent or adult. The aim of transactional analysis is to help clients to live more frequently in the 'adult' state.

SIX CATEGORY INTERVENTION ANALYSIS

This heuristic approach to classifying counselling and therapeutic interventions was developed by John Heron, a British philosopher and humanistic facilitator at the Human Potential Research Project, University of Surrey, Guildford (Heron 1975, 1990). He argued that all counselling interventions could be identified within the following six categories:

- Prescriptive interventions
- Informative interventions
- Confronting interventions
- Cathartic interventions
- Catalytic interventions
- Supportive interventions

COUNSELLING SKILLS

- Listening
- Reflection of feeling
- Reflection of content
- Challenging
- Coping with feelings
- Starting and ending the relationship
- Timing
- Giving information
- Supporting

STAGES IN THE COUNSELLING PROCESS

- Getting started
- Introductory talk
- Identifying the issues
- Coping with feelings

- Identifying possible solutions
- Agreeing a plan
- Implementing the plan

METHODS OF LEARNING COUNSELLING

- Counselling-skills workshops
- Certificate, diploma and masters degree courses
- Reading and private study
- On the job
- Sitting with Nellie: observing other counsellors at work
- Teaching yourself
- Correspondence courses (believe it or not, there are at least two counselling-skills correspondence courses in the UK!)
- Use of videos, tapes and films
- Attendance at weekend workshops
- Specialist courses
- In-house training
- Undergoing personal therapy and/or counselling

ELEMENTS OF COUNSELLING-SKILLS TRAINING

- *Theory input.* All counselling training should be supported by adequate reference to the relevant research and theory.
- *Self-exploration.* Those training as counsellors should, at least minimally, be prepared to explore their own beliefs, values, thoughts and feelings if they plan to help other people to explore theirs.
- *Skills framework.* Identifying a range of counselling skills within a framework makes learning the skills more manageable. Heron's Six Category Intervention Analysis referred to in this chapter and elsewhere is an example of one such framework.
- *Skills rehearsal.* Practising skills in the supportive company of others can help in the development of a range of counselling skills. The activities described in this book are an example of this

approach in practice. Another name for it is *micro-skills training*.

- *Reflecting on performance*. In all workshops there should be periods in which trainees think about their own counselling skills, their personal style and their aims.
- *Relating practice to theory*. Clear links need to be made between the counselling skills that are practised and the descriptions of counselling theory as they appear in the literature. Practice without theory is aimless and theory without practice can make the enterprise purely academic.
- *Application to real life*. It is essential that the skills rehearsed in counselling-skills workshops are translated into real life as soon as possible. If they are not, the workshop will appear as an interesting 'island' in the middle of real life: it will not reflect real life itself.
- *Continuing development and education*. Learning to counsel, like any sort of learning, is a lifelong process. All the skills cannot be learned in one go. Also, counsellors tend to modify their approach as they develop as people.

SOME DON'TS IN COUNSELLING

- Don't moralize.
- Don't constantly compare the client's experience with your own.
- Don't offer advice on personal and emotional issues.
- Don't tell the client they *don't* feel a certain way (eg 'Of course you are not depressed').

EFFECTIVE LISTENING BEHAVIOURS IN COUNSELLING (after Egan 1990)

- Sitting squarely in relation to the client.
- Maintaining an open position with arms and legs uncrossed.
- Leaning slightly towards the client.
- Maintaining comfortable eye contact.
- Keeping a relaxed position.

WHAT TO DO IF THINGS GO WRONG

- Don't panic.
- Continue to listen to the client.
- Suggest that someone else be brought into the relationship.
- Ensure that you know where the client is going after the counselling interview.
- If you are very worried, telephone for help.
- Always keep a list of the telephone numbers of other helping agencies.

WHEN TO REFER ON

- When the client talks of suicide.
- When the client is obviously mentally ill.
- When the practical issues under discussion are ones that you know little about (eg legal issues).
- When you feel out of your depth and unable to help any further.

DATA PROTECTION ACT

If you keep personal details about clients on a computer or in note form, you must register under the Data Protection Act. There are eight general principles behind the act.

- Personal data must be collected and used fairly without deceiving those concerned.
- Personal data must be registered under the Act.
- If you are going to pass on personal data to other people you must state this when you register.
- You should not keep more personal data than you need.
- You have to try to make sure that personal data is accurate and up to date.
- You should not keep personal data for longer than you need to.
- If you hold personal data about somebody, they have the right to know what it is and to check that it is accurate.

- You have to try to make sure that personal data is not changed, destroyed or disclosed without authorization (Branscombe 1991).

SELF-AWARENESS METHODS

In counselling, as in any form of therapeutic enterprise, it is important that you develop self-awareness – awareness of your own thoughts, feelings, attitudes, biases, aims, behaviours and your effect on other people. There are many ways of developing such an awareness and the process is never ending. Here are some self-awareness methods:

- Attendance at workshops and training courses
- Counselling as a client
- Co-counselling
- Meditation
- Reflection
- Keeping a journal or diary
- Discussion with peers and friends
- Inviting feedback from others
- Listening to others
- Noticing moods, thoughts, behaviours, etc
- Comparing self with others
- Regular self-appraisal
- Stress-management methods
- Psychotherapy
- Analysis

BASIC COUNSELLING READING LIST

There are various books listed in the reference and bibliography sections at the end of the book. Here, though, is a short list of books that will be useful as pre-workshop or pre-course reading material:

Burnard, P. (1989) *Counselling Skills for Health Professionals*, Chapman & Hall, London.

Claxton, G. (1984) *Live and Learn, An Introduction to the Psychology of Growth and Change in Everyday Life*, Harper & Row, London.

Dryden, W., Charles-Edwards, D. and Woolfe, R. (1989) *Handbook of Counselling in Britain*, Routledge.

Egan, G. (1990) *The Skilled Helper* (4th edn), Brooks/Cole, Pacific Grove, CA.

Heron, J. (1990) *Helping the Client*, Sage, London.

Munro, A., Manthei, B. and Small, J. (1988) *Counselling, The Skills of Problem-Solving*, Routledge, London.

Murgatroyd, S. (1986) *Counselling and Helping*, British Psychological Society and Methuen, London.

Nelson-Jones, R. (1981) *The Theory and Practice of Counselling Psychology*, Holt Rinehart & Winston, London.

(1984) *Personal Responsibility: Counselling and Therapy: an Integrative Approach*, Harper & Row, London.

Reddy, M. (1987) *The Manager's Guide to Counselling at Work*, Methuen, London.

Rogers, C.R. (1967) *On Becoming a Person*, Constable, London.

Summary checklist
1. What would *you* add to the checklists?
2. What else do you need to learn about the *theory* of counselling?
3. What do you identify as the most important *skills* of counselling?

Chapter 5:

Counselling-skills training checklists

AIMS OF THE CHAPTER

This chapter offers checklists on a variety of aspects of counselling skills training. Many of the theoretical and practical issues related to running counselling-skills workshops have been discussed. This chapter summarizes some of the principles and illustrates their use. It offers an account of the things to think about when running a workshop and can be used as a further checklist of considerations to be made when planning and working with groups. Some of the issues identified in the checklists of the previous chapter are consolidated here.

QUESTIONS TO ASK YOURSELF BEFORE YOU RUN A COUNSELLING-SKILLS WORKSHOP

- Have you identified a clear demand for a counselling-skills workshop?
- Are you sure that it will be cost effective?
- Are you happy to run the workshop on your own or do you need a co-trainer to work with you?

● Are you satisfied that you can successfully negotiate some of the content of the workshop with the trainees? If so, is it likely that you will be able to meet their needs or will you have to 'buy in' help from elsewhere?

BEFORE YOU START

First of all, the workshop has to be planned. You need to give consideration to the following teaching and learning issues:

● What are the aims of your workshop?
● What content will you include?
● What teaching and learning methods will you use?
● How will you evaluate the workshop?

Counselling Skills Training Workshop January 19th 1998		
Time	Activities	Notes
9.00	Registration and coffee	● check coffee ● take registration sheet ● check OHP ● remember handouts, OHP, acetates and notes.
9.30 - 10.00	Introduction to trainer and introductory activity	Icebreaker 2
10.00 - 10.30	Theory input: Counselling skills in the health care setting	● Handouts ● OHPs ● Notes
10.30 - 11.00	Coffee	Check coffee
11.00 - 12.30	Listening exercise	Activity 9
12.30 - 1.00	Lunch	Don't forget to confirm 15 extra lunches
1.00 - 2.00	Exercise in using basic counselling skills	Activity 12
2.00 - 3.00	Exercise applying counselling skills to everyday working practice	Activity 19
3.00 - 3.30	Tea	Check tea
3.30 - 4.00	Open discussion	
4.00 - 4.30	Evaluation of workshop Distribution of booklists and handouts	● Self and peer evaluation format ● Remember handouts

Figure 5.1 Example trainer's timetable

Once you have clarified these issues, work out a timetable of events for the day. Remember that it is easy to overestimate the amount of ground that you can cover in one day. Figure 5.1 is an illustration of a possible timetable for a one-day workshop on counselling skills. The timetable is for use by the trainer.

Alongside these educational issues, you will need to consider these domestic issues:

- How many people will be attending your workshop?
- Have they all had clear joining instructions?
- Have they all paid their fees?
- Have you booked rooms for the workshop?
- Have you all the equipment that you need?
- Have you made arrangements for tea, coffee and meal breaks?
- Have you had programmes printed and have they been sent to participants? Do you have some spares?

BEFORE THE PARTICIPANTS ARRIVE

On the day of the workshop, you will need to arrive early and check the following:

- The seating arrangements. It is useful to sit participants and yourself in a closed circle of chairs. In this formation, everyone can see everyone else and no one dominates the proceedings.
- The heating and ventilation of the room.
- Is there a rule about smoking? If participants are to be allowed to smoke, is provision made for seating them separately to non-smokers and are there enough ash trays?
- Does all your equipment work? If you are using an overhead projector, check that you have spare bulbs and that you know how to change them. If you are using flipchart pads, make sure that you have enough. Also, make sure that your flipchart marker pens all work.
- If necessary, turn on any heating systems for tea and coffee.
- Make sure that you have a list of the participants and have some means of checking names as people arrive. One way to do this is to have people sign their names on a pre-printed form.

OPENING THE WORKSHOP

The workshop should start promptly, at the time given on the programme. When latecomers arrive, greet them and ask them to assimilate themselves into the group. At the first break, invite them to introduce themselves to the group.

When you open the workshop, consider the following order of events:

- First, introduce yourself. Remember that your introduction will serve as an example of the way that other people will introduce themselves.
- Next, use one of the introductory icebreakers or exercises on the following pages to enable people to get to know each other.
- Once you are satisfied that most people know who they are sharing the room with, clarify the aims of the workshop, announce any domestic details about breaks and then outline the structure of the day.

EXAMPLE ICEBREAKERS

Icebreaker 1

Aim of icebreaker: To encourage people in a group to get to know each other.

Number of participants: any number between 5 and 25.

Environment: A large room in which people can sit comfortably in a group. Chairs should be of equal height and the group should remain in a closed circle throughout the activity. The trainer should be part of that circle.

Instructions: Each person, in turn, tells the rest of the group the following things:

- their name
- their job

- where they live
- two of three things about themselves

The group trainer joins in the activity wherever possible.

Icebreaker 2

Aim of icebreaker: To encourage all members of a workshop or course to get to know each other.

Number of participants: any number between 5 and 25.

Environment: A large room with chairs of equal height. Space enough to allow participants to pair off and then to reconvene. Smaller rooms can be used for the pairs activity, as required.

Instructions: After a brief self-introduction to the group, the trainer asks the participants to pair off with someone in the room that they do not know. The pairs then interview each other for about 10 minutes. Once all the interviews have been completed, the larger group reforms. Each person, in turn, stands behind the person he or she interviewed and introduces that person to the group. If there is an odd number of participants, the trainer makes up a pair. If not, then further personal details are offered after all the feedback to the larger group has taken place.

Icebreaker 3

Aim of icebreaker: To ensure that people get to know each other and to encourage group cohesion.

Number of participants: any number between 5 and 25.

Environment: A large room in which people can sit comfortably in a group. Chairs should be of equal height and the group should remain in a closed circle throughout the activity. The trainer should be part of that circle.

Instructions: After an initial welcome by the trainer, participants are asked to stand up, mill around the room and, at a given signal from the trainer, stop and introduce themselves to the person nearest to them. The process is then repeated until group members have met and shaken hands with everyone else in the room. Once the larger group reconvenes, it is helpful if each person is also invited to re-introduce themselves to the group by stating their name. The group trainer joins in the activity wherever possible.

A THEORY INPUT

Many people like to start counselling skills workshops with a brief theory input in order to offer a framework for participants to hang their ideas on. If you choose to do things this way, have your theory input well prepared, use plenty of visual aids and keep the presentation short and simple. Resist the tendency to lecture and try to make sure that all participants take part in the discussion of the main points of your input. Alternatively, avoid a theory input altogether and go straight into one or more of the counselling skills activities. You can relate practice to theory later in the day.

INTRODUCING EXERCISES AND ACTIVITIES

There are a number of factors to bear in mind when using counselling-skills activities and exercises:

- Allow plenty of time. Do not try to cram too many activities into too short a space of time. The reflection period of the activity and the discussion of it is usually more important than the activity itself. It is during this phase that the experiential learning cycle is being completed. People are making sense of what has happened to them. Allow about one hour for each activity.
- Make sure that you give clear instructions about the activity. Check that everyone in the room is clear about what you are asking them to do. If necessary, write out the instructions and give them to participants as a handout. This is particularly important if you are working with large groups.
- Stick to the format of the activity. Once you have given

instructions, follow them yourself. Resist the temptation to modify the exercise once it is underway.

- Keep to time. If you suggest that part of an activity will take five minutes to complete, remind participants when the five minutes are up.
- If you are using a pairs activity, be authoritative when you ask the group to reconvene. Sit in the larger circle of chairs and call participants to join you. Once you have called them back, remain silent until everyone is back in the larger group.

REFLECTION AND PROCESSING

The reflection and discussion after an activity are the most important elements of the undertaking. Allow plenty of time for discussion. Begin the discussion with a broad open question such as 'What happened?', 'What did you notice?' or 'How did you feel about the exercise?'

Allow participants plenty of time to think about what you have asked and let people respond in their own time. Avoid the 'school-teacher' approach of making a point of asking each person, in turn, to respond. If people choose not to respond to the question, this should be respected. Try to avoid pre-emptive questions such as: 'Did you notice how . . . ?' and 'Did anyone feel that . . . ?'

Accept the fact that participants will respond to the activities idiosyncratically. It is important that people are allowed to verbalize what happened to *them* and that they are not rushed to see the outcome of an activity in a particular sort of way. On the other hand, encourage participants to link their experiences with the 'real world' with questions such as: 'What are the implications of all this. . .?', 'How does all this link up with your job . . .?' or 'What are the key issues here . . .?'

TAKING BREAKS

Try to gauge the atmosphere and the rhythm of the group. Do not carry on when people are obviously flagging. Take regular, short breaks. Such breaks can be an important part of the learning process as this is the time that people 'really' talk to each other. If the atmosphere flags a little between breaks, consider running a quick icebreaker or revitalizing activity.

HANDOUTS AND BOOKLISTS

If necessary, prepare handouts that contain further reading, booklists and other information. Try to make sure that these are professionally prepared using a wordprocessor, desktop publishing program and a laser printer. If you use a desktop publishing program, keep your design simple, do not use too many founts (print faces) and try to establish a uniform look to the handouts that you use. Do not prepare handouts that contain too much information. Three-page, closely printed handouts are rarely read. A single side of A4, on the other hand, can be read quickly and may well spark off further discussion.

CLOSING THE WORKSHOP

Consider, carefully, the closing activity that you use. Such activities may be of various kinds:

- activities which help to evaluate the workshop;
- activities which enable participants to evaluate their own performance;
- activities which encourage people to link their learning to 'real life';
- activities which enable participants to say goodbye to each other.

Summary checklist

1. What other checklists would *you* look for in thinking about running workshops?

2. How did you learn to run groups?

3. What sorts of skills are needed by trainers who run 'training-the-trainers' workshops?

Chapter 6:

Introduction to the activities

AIMS OF THE CHAPTER

This chapter focuses on:

- how to use the activities in this manual;
- icebreakers and introductions;
- what to do if things go wrong;
- debriefing;
- application to real life.

HOW TO USE THE ACTIVITIES

The following chapters offer a range of activities for counselling skills training. They can be worked through in order, or the trainer can select various activities from each section. Each chapter covers a different set of activities, as follows:

- Listening activities.
- Empathy-building activities.
- Information and advice-giving activities.

- Facilitation activities.
- Problem-solving activities.
- Coping with feelings.
- Evaluation activities.
- Counsellor-development activities.

Each activity is self-contained and can be used as it stands. Full instructions are given for each activity. Each one has sections on:

- Title of the activity.
- Activity number.
- Time required for the activity.
- Aim of the activity.
- Number of participants.
- Environment.
- Instructions.
- Evaluation procedure.
- Closing the activity.

It is most important that each activity is worked through slowly. The aim should always be to encourage trainees to notice what is happening to them and to reflect on the process afterwards. Each of the activities offers a structure for people to be able to do this. The process of learning counselling skills is not simply one of practising a series of behaviours until they are practised perfectly. Each trainee and each trainer brings their own style to a particular aspect of counselling. This individual 'tailoring' is important. The aim is not to produce clones but to encourage people actively to think about their behaviour in order to make it more effective.

ICEBREAKERS AND INTRODUCTIONS

Icebreakers or warm-up exercises are useful for getting people into the mood for activity-based work. Three examples were given in Chapter 5 and others can be found elsewhere. People vary in their reaction to icebreakers. In my experience, some people enjoy taking part in them while others object on the grounds that they feel a bit silly. Some icebreakers mimic children's games and these may not be appropriate for use with more mature groups. On the other hand, such activities can sometimes be useful in breaking down barriers and encouraging people to loosen up a little. The best thing is for the trainer to pay attention to the apparent needs and wants of the group and to respect any suggestion either that icebreakers be avoided or that such activities would be helpful. Most people taking part in counselling-skills workshops will already have had some experience of introductory exercises and therefore can easily make their mind up about whether or not they would be appropriate for any particular set of circumstances.

WHAT TO DO IF THINGS GO WRONG

Group work does not always run to plan. Things can go wrong. Some of the things that can happen are that:

- some people feel that progress is too slow;
- someone gets angry as a result of something that is said;
- some people get embarrassed as a result of an activity or discussion;
- someone makes a suggestion that no one takes up and that person gets offended as a result;
- activities over- or under-run.

There are some general principles that can be used to cope with these and other problems in groups. Although all groups are different, many of the strategies and interventions used by trainers can be applied to a wide range of situations. Here are some of them:

- As the trainer, notice what is happening in the group.
- Ask group members to comment on what is happening in the group.
- Institute a 'negotiation' clause, early in the life of the group. This is introduced by the trainer stating something along the lines of:

   At any time during the life of this group, any group member should feel free to propose any change that they would like to see in what is happening in the group. That proposal will then be put to the rest of the group and the group's decision will be binding until another proposal is forthcoming.

- Allow people to 'sit out' of activities that they do not wish to take part in. Counselling-skills training is a form of adult education and no one should feel compelled to take part in activities. Insisting on participation rarely works, anyway. A person who begrudgingly takes part in an activity rarely learns very much from it. Paradoxically, if people are allowed complete licence, they very often join in everything.
- Go easy on yourself. Do not work too hard at being the perfect trainer. Admit it if you make an error of judgement and try to make sure that all *major* decisions are negotiated rather than unilaterally imposed.
- Allow for fairly frequent breaks. Do not allow a 'hothouse' atmosphere to develop. The aim is not to run a *therapy* group but a *training* one. No one should feel that the atmosphere is becoming too emotional or oppressive.

DEBRIEFING

All the activities in this book call on people's personal experience. Whenever we disclose things about ourselves (beyond the obvious), we invest some emotion in what we are doing. It often takes courage to talk about ourselves and our experience in the company of other people. Sometimes, too, feelings get stirred up. It is important, therefore, that at the end of each activity some time is spent in discussing what people felt about doing the activity. This period is known as debriefing time. In role play, the term has a slightly different meaning. The debriefing time following role play is a time in which people disassociate themselves from the roles they have been playing. For example, the student who has been role playing a senior manager, is allowed to 'return' to his everyday and 'real' role. Sometimes, people have difficulty in this sort of return. The following statements can help:

Just spend a few moments coming back from your role as — to who you are in everyday life. It may help if you just tell us your name and what you normally do when you are not attending work-shops like this . . .

Different trainers have different views about the importance of the debriefing period. Some feel that it is useful to allow a person to continue to muse over the role that they have been playing and not particularly helpful to make sure that a person is 'brought back'. Others feel just as strongly that it is vital that a person is returned to their normal role. Give this issue considerable thought and decide, in the light of your own experience, which side you come down on. You may decide, on the other hand, that sometimes you need to use a debriefing approach, while on other occasions it is not necessary. If you can, attend other trainers' workshops and see what they do.

APPLICATION OF LEARNING TO REAL LIFE

Transfer of learning is an important aspect of running counselling skills workshops. It is of little value if people learn skills in workshops which they do not use in everyday life. One persistent theme through any workshop should be the exhortation that the trainees try out the skills they have learned in situations away from the workshop. One simple application of this idea is to remind trainees to use such skills 'tonight'. Then, in the morning (or on the next day of the workshop), trainees can be invited to report back on how they used the skills at home, in the pub, at a meeting and so on.

The other approach to ensuring that skills are applied in real life is to organize a 'recall' day as described in Chapter 2. Such a day can be held about two months after the first workshop and trainees can be asked to discuss, in small groups, the ways in which they have applied what they learnt there. Other issues that can be identified in such follow-up days are:

- further counselling theory;
- problems encountered;
- difficult counselling scenarios;
- further training needs.

WORKING WITH LARGER GROUPS

Most of the activities in the next chapters can be used with more than 25 participants if a certain amount of structure is used. One way of managing larger numbers is to draw up a handout that gives explicit instructions to participants. Then, sub-groups from the larger group are nominated and a chairperson for each of the sub-groups is elected. The task of each chairperson is to work through the instructions sheet with their group and to ensure the smooth running of the activity. After the activity has been run through in each of the sub-groups, the larger group reforms. The chairperson feeds back to that larger group during the plenary session. Structure is essential if the serial working of sub-groups is to be effective. Make sure that everyone is clear about the aims of the activity and what it is that they are supposed to be doing.

Headings for an instruction sheet might be as follows:

- Title of the activity
- Aims of the activity
- What to do
- The role of the chairperson

Activities checklist
1. Are you confident about using 'activities' as part of a counselling skills training package?
2. What will *you* do if things go wrong?
3. How will you evaluate the learning that takes place in your workshop or course?

PART II

TRAINING ACTIVITIES

Chapter 7:

Listening activities

POSITIVE LISTENING BEHAVIOURS

Activity 1

Time required 45 minutes to 1 hour.

Aim To explore effective listening behaviours.

Group size Any number between 5 and 25.

Environment A room in which there is space for everyone to sit in a closed circle of chairs and which is large enough for everyone to pair off and spread out, if required. There should be a flipchart and pad or a white/blackboard and marker pens. This is used to jot down comments from group members during discussion periods. Flipchart sheets containing such comments can be pinned to the wall to act as an *aide mémoire*. These can be kept on the wall until the end of the workshop and they help to maintain continuity of content and demonstrate progress.

You may want to present any theoretical points on an acetate sheet, in which case an overhead projector and screen will be required. Any handouts should be prepared prior to using this activity and it is important that there are enough for each person to have one. Reading lists can be given out at the end of the activity and these should be no more than one page long.

Keep the activity brisk and the discussion lively. Allow everyone to have their say.

Procedure Trainees pair off and sit in their pairs, facing one another. One person is designated the 'listener' and the other the 'talker'. All the listeners are given the handout and asked to observe the SOLER behaviours contained in it. They are asked to sit squarely, maintain an open position, lean slightly towards the other person and relax.

The talker, in each pair, then talks to the other person on one or more of the following topics:

- interests away from work;
- music;
- holidays.

The listeners in each pair do just that. The aim is to explore the process of listening while demonstrating effective listening behaviours. After 10 minutes, the pairs switch roles; the talkers become the listeners and vice versa for a further 10 minutes.

At the end of the second 10 minutes, the larger group is reconvened and the trainer initiates a discussion on the trainees' observations from undertaking the activity. The trainer joins in this activity if there is an odd number of participants.

Evaluation Two 'rounds' are conducted. In the first round, each person in turn says what they liked *least* about the activity. In the second, each person in turn says what they liked *most* about the activity. The trainer joins in this evaluation process and decides whether or not there is a discussion of the points that are raised.

Closing Participants should be offered a 5-minute period in which to raise questions, express feelings, address particular people in the group or talk through anything else that has arisen from the activity.

LISTENING BEHAVIOURS

The following 'SOLER' behaviours tend to demonstrate the fact that you are listening. Use them as a 'baseline' for monitoring your own behaviour during counselling.

- Sitting squarely
- Open position
- Leaning forward
- Eye contact
- Relaxing

Source: Egan, G. (1990) *The Skilled Helper* (4th edn), Brooks/Cole, Pacific Grove, CA.

NEGATIVE LISTENING BEHAVIOURS
Activity 2

Time required 45 minutes to 1 hour.

Aim To explore ineffective listening behaviours.

Group size Any number between 5 and 25.

Environment A room in which there is space for everyone to sit in a closed circle of chairs and which is large enough for everyone to pair off and spread out, if required. There should be a flipchart and pad or a white/blackboard and marker pens. This is used to jot down comments from group members during discussion periods. Flipchart sheets containing such comments can be pinned to the wall to act as an *aide mémoire*. These can be kept on the wall until the end of the workshop and they help to maintain continuity of content and demonstrate progress.

You may want to present any theoretical points on an acetate sheet, in which case an overhead projector and screen will be required. Any handouts should be prepared prior to using this activity and it is important that there are enough for each person to have one. Reading lists can be given out at the end of the activity and these should be no more than one page long.

Allow everyone to speak and wait until all thoughts and feelings have been shared in the group before moving on to another activity.

Procedure Trainees pair off and sit in their pairs, facing one another. One person is designated the 'listener' and the other the 'talker'. Each 'listener' is given the handout on negative listening behaviours and asked to enact them during the next few minutes. The 'talker' in each pair then talks about one or more of the following topics:

- things that cause me stress;
- the happiest period of my life;
- hobbies and interests.

During the time that the talker is talking, the 'listener' observes all the negative behaviour on the handout but, at the same time *listens to the other person*. The aim of this exercise is to explore what it feels like to be listened to when the other person does not *appear* to be listening. This continues for 10 minutes after which time the pairs switch roles for a further 10 minutes. During that time, the listener talks and the talker listens – observing the negative listening behaviours.

After a further 10 minutes, the larger group is reconvened and the trainer initiates a discussion on what it felt like to be listened to when the listener did not display the appropriate behaviours. The trainer takes part in the activity wherever possible.

Evaluation Each person in turn says what they learnt from the activity and what they will take with them back to 'real life', away from the group.

Closing Participants should be offered a 5-minute period in which to raise questions, express feelings, address particular people in the group or talk through anything else that has arisen from the activity.

NEGATIVE LISTENING BEHAVIOURS

In this exercise, you are required to REVERSE most of Egan's positive listening behaviours (see Activity 1). During the exercise:

- DO NOT sit squarely
- DO NOT maintain open position
- DO NOT lean forward
- DO NOT maintain eye contact

Source: Egan, G. (1990) *The Skilled Helper* (4th edn), Brooks/Cole, Pacific Grove, CA.

PROXIMITY IN LISTENING

Activity 3

Time required 45 minutes to 1 hour.

Aim To explore territory, personal space and distance between listeners and talkers.

Group size Any number between 5 and 25.

Environment A room in which there is space for everyone to sit in a closed circle of chairs and which is large enough for everyone to pair off and spread out, if required. There should be a flipchart and pad or a white/blackboard and marker pens. This is used to jot down comments from group members during discussion periods. Flipchart sheets containing such comments can be pinned to the wall to act as an *aide mémoire*. These can be kept on the wall until the end of the workshop and they help to maintain continuity of content and demonstrate progress.

You may want to present any theoretical points on an acetate sheet, in which case an overhead projector and screen will be required. Any handouts should be prepared prior to using this activity and it is important that there are enough for each person to have one. Reading lists can be given out at the end of the activity and these should be no more than one page long.

Encourage everyone to discuss the activity afterwards and make sure that everyone who wants to say something gets the chance.

Procedure Trainees pair off and sit in their pairs, facing one another. Each pair is given one of the handouts that follow these instructions. Then, each pair works through the instructions on the sheet and explores the issue of proximity in listening. Thus they:

- Sit very close to each other, with their knees almost touching.
- Sit at least five feet away from each other.
- Sit side by side.
- Sit back to back.
- Sit next to each other.
- Sit facing each other at a comfortable distance.

They are asked to hold a conversation, in each of these positions, for about 5 minutes. Topics for these discussions can include:

- Times when I have felt really listened-to.
- People who I think are good listeners.
- The difficulties of listening to another person.
- Personal space.

When all participants have worked through all the above combinations, the larger group is reconvened and the trainer initiates a discussion about the issues of proximity and personal space in counselling. The trainer takes part in this activity as part of one of the pairs.

Evaluation The group is divided into pairs and each pair spends 5 minutes discussing what each person liked and disliked about the activity. The group reforms after 5 minutes and an evaluative discussion is held.

Closing Participants should be offered a 5-minute period in which to raise questions, express feelings, address particular people in the group or talk through anything else that has arisen from the activity.

PROXIMITY EXERCISE

In this exercise, you will be exploring PROXIMITY in the counselling relationship. Once you have paired off, experiment with sitting with your partner by adopting the following positions. Continue to discuss the topic given to you by the trainer throughout this activity and note the differences that various types of proximity make.

- Sit very close to each other, with your knees almost touching.
- Sit at least five feet away from each other.
- Sit side by side.
- Sit back to back.
- Sit next to each other.
- Sit facing each other at a comfortable distance.

USING SILENCE
Activity 4

Time required 45 minutes to 1 hour.

Aim To enable trainees to explore eye contact and silence.

Group size Any number between 5 and 25.

Environment A room in which there is space for everyone to sit in a closed circle of chairs and which is large enough for everyone to pair off and spread out, if required. There should be a flipchart and pad or a white/blackboard and marker pens. This is used to jot down comments from group members during discussion periods. Flipchart sheets containing such comments can be pinned to the wall to act as an *aide mémoire*. These can be kept on the wall until the end of the workshop and they help to maintain continuity of content and demonstrate progress.

You may want to present any theoretical points on an acetate sheet, in which case an overhead projector and screen will be required. Any handouts should be prepared prior to using this activity and it is important that there are enough for each person to have one. Reading lists can be given out at the end of the activity and these should be no more than one page long.

Do not hurry people but keep the atmosphere in the group lively and encourage people to share their thoughts and feelings about the activity.

Procedure Trainees pair off and sit opposite one another. They sit for 5 minutes in complete silence and experiment with the following:

- Maintaining full eye contact.
- Making no eye contact at all.
- Changing facial expression.

During this 5-minute period, the trainees should be aware of how they are feeling about what is happening. They should notice the following:

- What feels comfortable about the silence.
- What feels uncomfortable.
- What behaviours seemed to make the silence more uncomfortable.
- The point at which they feel compelled to look away from their partners.

After the 5-minute period, the trainees remain in their pairs and discuss the activity. They explore the degree to which *they* use silence in counselling relationships and the difficulties (or otherwise) that they have with silence. They should note, particularly, if they tend to find that they are 'sentence finishers' for other people. They should try, too, to identify exactly what it is that makes silence difficult for them. Then they should discuss how silence might be therapeutic or beneficial in a counselling relationship.

After a further 10 minutes, the larger group is reconvened and the trainer initiates a discussion about the activity and attempts to draw out both the negative and positive aspects of silence in counselling. Particularly, the group should address the question of the *value* of silence in counselling – particularly on the part of the counsellor. It is arguable that in the most effective counselling, the counsellor will remain silent for much of the session. The trainer joins in this activity if there is an odd number of participants.

Evaluation Each person in the group makes notes about what they found useful about the activity. Then an evaluative discussion is held with the trainer as facilitator of that discussion.

Closing Participants should be offered a 5-minute period in which to raise questions, express feelings, address particular people in the group or talk through anything else that has arisen from the activity.

HEAD NODDING
Activity 5

Time required 45 minutes to 1 hour.

Aim To explore one particular element of non-verbal communication – head nodding.

Group size Any number between 5 and 25.

Environment A room in which there is space for everyone to sit in a closed circle of chairs and which is large enough for everyone to pair off and spread out, if required. There should be a flipchart and pad or a white/blackboard and marker pens. This is used to jot down comments from group members during discussion periods. Flipchart sheets containing such comments can be pinned to the wall to act as an *aide mémoire*. These can be kept on the wall until the end of the workshop and they help to maintain continuity of content and demonstrate progress.

You may want to present any theoretical points on an acetate sheet, in which case an overhead projector and screen will be required. Any handouts should be prepared prior to using this activity and it is important that there are enough for each person to have one. Reading lists can be given out at the end of the activity and these should be no more than one page long.

Encourage everyone to discuss the activity afterwards and make sure that everyone who wants to say something gets the chance.

Procedure This is an activity which highlights one particular aspect of non-verbal communication – one that is often taken for granted.

Trainees are invited to pair off. One of each pair is the 'talker' and the other the 'listener'. Talkers then talk to the listeners for about 5 minutes on a topic of their choice. While they are talking, the listeners experiment with nodding their heads. Thus, they work through the following combinations:

- Almost continual head nodding.
- No head nodding at all.
- Occasional but exaggerated head nodding.
- 'Normal' head nodding.

This activity is useful for helping people to appreciate the degree to which they 'automatically' nod their heads while listening in a counselling relationship. It is all too easy to get caught up in what might be called the 'dog in the back of the car' syndrome. The point of this activity is to enable participants to *choose* the amount of nodding they do and to bring that activity under conscious control.

After 5 minutes, roles are reversed and the listeners become talkers. The new listeners then work through the list of possibilities. After the second 5-minute period, the trainees stay in their pairs and discuss the activity for a further 10 minutes. During this time, they may or may not be prompted by the trainer to notice the amount of head nodding they use in the discussion.

When the pairs' discussions have finished, the larger group reconvenes and the trainer leads a discussion on the whole of the activity and on the value or otherwise of head nodding while listening. The trainer takes part in the activity wherever possible.

Evaluation The group is divided into pairs and each pair spends 5 minutes discussing what each person liked and disliked about the activity. The group reforms after 5 minutes and an evaluative discussion is held.

Closing Participants should be offered a 5-minute period in which to raise questions, express feelings, address particular people in the group or talk through anything else that has arisen from the activity.

FACIAL EXPRESSION
Activity 6

Time required 45 minutes to 1 hour.

Aim To explore elements of facial expression during listening.

Group size Any number between 5 and 25.

Environment A room in which there is space for everyone to sit in a closed circle of chairs and which is large enough for everyone to pair off and spread out, if required. There should be a flipchart and pad or a white/blackboard and marker pens. This is used to jot down comments from group members during discussion periods. Flipchart sheets containing such comments can be pinned to the wall to act as an *aide mémoire*. These can be kept on the wall until the end of the workshop and they help to maintain continuity of content and demonstrate progress.

You may want to present any theoretical points on an acetate sheet, in which case an overhead projector and screen will be required. Any handouts should be prepared prior to using this activity and it is important that there are enough for each person to have one. Reading lists can be given out at the end of the activity and these should be no more than one page long.

Keep the activity brisk and the discussion lively. Allow everyone to have their say.

Procedure Group members pair off and sit facing one another. They then hold a conversation on any topic of their choice and 'experiment' with their facial expression by working through the following list:

- They maintain a 'blank' expression for 5 minutes.
- They exaggerate their facial expression as they listen.

- They increase their amount of blinking.
- They hold their head on one side.
- They change the position of their head.
- They maintain a 'normal' facial expression.

Each facial expression or position of the head should be maintained for about 3 or 4 minutes. The various combinations can either be worked through by one person at a time or simultaneously by both parties. The aim is to identify which facial expressions are helpful in the listening process and which are a hindrance.

This activity can generate a lot of amusement and it is important to allow people to work through their embarrassment by laughing a little. Usually, most people settle down and find the activity both useful and thought-provoking. It is an exercise which helps to heighten awareness of taken-for-granted expressions and head positions.

When each pair has worked through the list of expressions, the larger group is reconvened and a discussion is initiated about the role and appropriateness of facial expression in counselling and in listening. The trainer joins in this activity if there is an odd number of participants.

Evaluation Each person in turn says what they learnt from the activity and what they will take with them back to 'real life', away from the group.

Closing Participants should be offered a 5-minute period in which to raise questions, express feelings, address particular people in the group or talk through anything else that has arisen from the activity.

ACTIVE LISTENING
Activity 7

Time required 45 minutes to 1 hour.

Aim To explore a range of elements of the listening process.

Group size Any number between 5 and 25.

Environment A room in which there is space for everyone to sit in a closed circle of chairs and which is large enough for everyone to pair off and spread out, if required. There should be a flipchart and pad or a white/blackboard and marker pens. This is used to jot down comments from group members during discussion periods. Flipchart sheets containing such comments can be pinned to the wall to act as an *aide mémoire*. These can be kept on the wall until the end of the workshop and they help to maintain continuity of content and demonstrate progress.

You may want to present any theoretical points on an acetate sheet, in which case an overhead projector and screen will be required. Any handouts should be prepared prior to using this activity and it is important that there are enough for each person to have one. Reading lists can be given out at the end of the activity and these should be no more than one page long.

Allow everyone to speak and wait until all thoughts and feelings have been shared in the group before moving on to another activity.

Procedure The group pairs off and each pair sits facing one another. One of the pair is designated 'listener' and the other 'talker'. The talkers then talk to the listeners who use *active listening skills* during their time as listener. They use the following interventions and strategies:

● They observe the SOLER behaviours, described in Activity 1: they sit squarely in relation to the other person, they maintain an

open position (without crossed arms or legs), they lean slightly towards the other person, they maintain comfortable eye contact and they relax.
* They use 'minimal prompts' to encourage the other person. Examples of such prompts are:
  appropriate head nodding;
  the use of 'mm' and 'yes';
  very occasional questions;
  full use of appropriate facial expression.

After 10 minutes, the talker gives the listener feedback about the effectiveness or otherwise of their listening. Then, the pairs swap roles: the listeners become talkers and vice versa. The activity is then repeated for a further 10 minutes. After that time, the talker again offers feedback on the listener's ability to demonstrate effective listening skills.

Once all pairs have worked through the above process, the larger group reconvenes and a discussion about active listening is initiated. Feedback is also elicited as to the relative levels of listening skills within the group and trainees are asked to comment on their *own* performances. The trainer takes part in this activity as part of one of the pairs.

Evaluation Two 'rounds' are conducted. In the first round, each person in turn says what they liked *least* about the activity. In the second, each person in turn says what they liked *most* about the activity. The trainer joins in this evaluation process and decides whether or not there is a discussion of the points that are raised.

Closing Participants should be offered a 5-minute period in which to raise questions, express feelings, address particular people in the group or talk through anything else that has arisen from the activity.

DISTRACTION
Activity 8

Time required 45 minutes to 1 hour.

Aim To explore distraction in the listening process.

Group size Any number between 5 and 25.

Environment A room in which there is space for everyone to sit in a closed circle of chairs and which is large enough for everyone to pair off and spread out, if required. There should be a flipchart and pad or a white/blackboard and marker pens. This is used to jot down comments from group members during discussion periods. Flipchart sheets containing such comments can be pinned to the wall to act as an *aide mémoire*. These can be kept on the wall until the end of the workshop and they help to maintain continuity of content and demonstrate progress.

You may want to present any theoretical points on an acetate sheet, in which case an overhead projector and screen will be required. Any handouts should be prepared prior to using this activity and it is important that there are enough for each person to have one. Reading lists can be given out at the end of the activity and these should be no more than one page long.

Encourage everyone to discuss the activity afterwards and make sure that everyone who wants to say something gets the chance.

Procedure Trainees pair off and sit opposite one another. The pairs talk to each other quietly and observe, at the same time, the following things:

- Distractions within the immediate environment (clocks, outside traffic, other participants, etc).
- Internal distractions (sudden thoughts, ideas, feelings, etc).

- Distractions caused by the *content* of the conversation (associations, embarrassments, etc).

These conversations need to be carried out slowly, quietly and thoughtfully. They demand considerable attention on the part of the participants but can be a very useful way of enhancing self-awareness and awareness of both internal and external environments.

After fifteen minutes, the larger group reconvenes and the trainer helps the group to identify the various sorts of distractions. These can be written onto a flipchart sheet or a black- or whiteboard. Once all participants have had the chance to identify what they see as distractions, the trainer initiates a discussion about the issue of how to cope with such distractions in the counselling process. The trainer joins in this activity if there is an odd number of participants.

Evaluation Each person in turn says what they learnt from the activity and what they will take with them back to 'real life', away from the group.

Closing Participants should be offered a 5-minute period in which to raise questions, express feelings, address particular people in the group or talk through anything else that has arisen from the activity.

QUALITIES OF THE EFFECTIVE LISTENER
Activity 9

Time required 45 minutes to 1 hour.

Aim To identify the qualities of an effective listener.

Group size Any number between 5 and 25.

Environment A room in which there is space for everyone to sit in a closed circle of chairs and which is large enough for everyone to pair off and spread out, if required. There should be a flipchart and pad or a white/blackboard and marker pens. This is used to jot down comments from group members during discussion periods. Flipchart sheets containing such comments can be pinned to the wall to act as an *aide mémoire*. These can be kept on the wall until the end of the workshop and they help to maintain continuity of content and demonstrate progress.

You may want to present any theoretical points on an acetate sheet, in which case an overhead projector and screen will be required. Any handouts should be prepared prior to using this activity and it is important that there are enough for each person to have one. Reading lists can be given out at the end of the activity and these should be no more than one page long.

Keep the activity brisk and the discussion lively. Allow everyone to have their say.

Procedure The group divides up into small groups of three of four. They are asked to 'brainstorm', on to a large sheet of paper, the personal qualities that they feel a good listener should have. There should be no limit imposed on the number of qualities that any group may identify but a distinction should be made between skills and qualities. Skills are things that people do, qualities are the personal characteristics that people have. The aim of this activity is to identify qualities. Here are some examples of such qualities identified by other groups that have undertaken this activity:

- sense of humour;
- personal warmth;
- being non-judgemental;
- being open;
- thoughtfulness;
- optimism;
- spontaneity;
- cheerful disposition;
- not moralistic.

Note that the grammar of the presentation is not important. It is much more useful that people identify a wide range of personal characteristics that they associate with being a good listener.

After 15 minutes, each sub-group presents their list to the rest of the group and the trainer initiates a discussion on the issue of personal qualities and listening. The trainer may also want to discuss whether group participants feel that people can be *TRAINED* in these qualities or if they feel that people are born with them.

The question of personal qualities in counselling is one that is referred to again and again in the counselling literature and should be seen as central to the training process. In the end, it would seem that the personal relationship between counsellor and client is far more important than any particular skills that the counsellor may have and use (see, for example, Rogers 1967, Egan 1990, Heron 1990, Burnard 1989). The trainer takes part in this activity as part of one of the pairs.

Evaluation Two 'rounds' are conducted. In the first round, each person in turn says what they liked *least* about the activity. In the second, each person in turn says what they liked *most* about the activity. The trainer joins in this evaluation process and decides whether or not there is a discussion of the points that are raised.

Closing Participants should be offered a 5-minute period in which to raise questions, express feelings, address particular people in the group or talk through anything else that has arisen from the activity.

ASSESSING YOUR OWN LISTENING

Activity 10

Time required 45 minutes to 1 hour.

Aim To help trainees to assess their own listening skills.

Group size Any number between 5 and 25.

Environment A room in which there is space for everyone to sit in a closed circle of chairs and which is large enough for everyone to pair off and spread out, if required. There should be a flipchart and pad or a white/blackboard and marker pens. This is used to jot down comments from group members during discussion periods. Flipchart sheets containing such comments can be pinned to the wall to act as an *aide mémoire*. These can be kept on the wall until the end of the workshop and they help to maintain continuity of content and demonstrate progress.

You may want to present any theoretical points on an acetate sheet, in which case an overhead projector and screen will be required. Any handouts should be prepared prior to using this activity and it is important that there are enough for each person to have one. Reading lists can be given out at the end of the activity and these should be no more than one page long.

Allow everyone to speak and wait until all thoughts and feelings have been shared in the group before moving on to another activity.

Procedure Each participant is given a copy of the following questionnaire. The completed questionnaires and the resultant findings can be processed in any one of the following ways:

● The questionnaire can be 'scored' and the findings collated. If this is the chosen method of processing, then each item in each element of the questionnaire is ascribed a number, as follows:

Strongly Agree	Agree	Don't Know	Disagree	Strongly Disagree	Leave Blank
1	2	3	4	5	

Each participant scores the questionnaire by placing a number in the 'leave blank' section of each item. Once this has been done, all the questionnaires can be collected and the trainer undertakes an analysis of the frequencies for each item in the questionnaire. Thus, for each question, it is possible to compute the number of people in the group who answered 'strongly agree', 'agree', 'don't know' and so on. This information can then be fed back to the trainees. If the group is small, no attempt should be made at turning the findings into percentages. Simple frequency counts are all that are required.

- The questionnaires can be discussed, in pairs, by the participants.
- The questionnaires can be used as the basis of a discussion about the need for further personal development and training.

Evaluation Each person in turn says what they learnt from the activity and what they will take with them back to 'real life', away from the group.

Closing Participants should be offered a 5-minute period in which to raise questions, express feelings, address particular people in the group or talk through anything else that has arisen from the activity.

LISTENING ASSESSMENT QUESTIONNAIRE

Read through each of the statements and then tick a box. You may strongly agree, agree, disagree or strongly disagree with each statement. You may also indicate that you 'don't know' about a particular item. Work fairly quickly through the statements; do not miss any out.

1. I consider myself an effective listener.

Strongly Agree	Agree	Don't Know	Disagree	Strongly Disagree	Leave Blank

2. I enjoy listening to other people.

Strongly Agree	Agree	Don't Know	Disagree	Strongly Disagree	Leave Blank

3. I find listening fairly difficult when I am tired.

Strongly Agree	Agree	Don't Know	Disagree	Strongly Disagree	Leave Blank

4. Most people can listen without any particular training.

Strongly Agree	Agree	Don't Know	Disagree	Strongly Disagree	Leave Blank

5. I find listening exercises difficult to take part in.

Strongly Agree	Agree	Don't Know	Disagree	Strongly Disagree	Leave Blank

6. I can only listen to people I like.

Strongly Agree	Agree	Don't Know	Disagree	Strongly Disagree	Leave Blank

7. Listening is an art as well as a skill.

Strongly Agree	Agree	Don't Know	Disagree	Strongly Disagree	Leave Blank

8. It is important to listen to what people 'really' mean when they speak.

Strongly Agree	Agree	Don't Know	Disagree	Strongly Disagree	Leave Blank

9. Reading people's non-verbal communication is as important as listening to them.

Strongly Agree	Agree	Don't Know	Disagree	Strongly Disagree	Leave Blank

10. I need more practice in listening.

Strongly Agree	Agree	Don't Know	Disagree	Strongly Disagree	Leave Blank

Chapter 8:

Empathy-building activities

CLARIFYING EMPATHY
Activity 11

Time required 45 minutes to 1 hour.

Aim of activity To explore the concept of empathy.

Group size Any number between 5 and 25.

Environment A room in which there is space for everyone to sit in a closed circle of chairs and which is large enough for everyone to pair off and spread out, if required. There should be a flipchart and pad or a white/blackboard and marker pens. This is used to jot down comments from group members during discussion periods. Flipchart sheets containing such comments can be pinned to the wall to act as an *aide mémoire*. These can be kept on the wall until the end of the workshop and they help to maintain continuity of content and demonstrate progress.

You may want to present any theoretical points on an acetate sheet, in which case an overhead projector and screen will be required. Any handouts should be prepared prior to using this activity and it is important that there are enough for each person to have one. Reading lists can be given out at the end of the activity and these should be no more than one page long.

Encourage everyone to discuss the activity afterwards and make sure that everyone who wants to say something gets the chance.

Procedure The group pairs off. Each pair discusses the concept of empathy by reviewing the following questions:

- What is the difference between empathy and sympathy?
- To what degree is it possible truly to empathize with another person?
- Who can you most easily empathize with?
- With whom would you find empathy difficult?

The pairs discuss the questions for 15 minutes and jot down notes about their findings. After 15 minutes, the group reconvenes. The trainer invites the pairs to feed back their findings and then generates a discussion on the question of empathy in counselling. A handout for distribution in this activity is included at the end of this section.

Evaluation The group is divided into pairs and each pair spends 5 minutes discussing what each person liked and disliked about the activity. The group reforms after 5 minutes and an evaluative discussion is held.

Closing Participants should be offered a 5-minute period in which to raise questions, express feelings, address particular people in the group or talk through anything else that has arisen from the activity.

EMPATHY EXERCISE

When you divide into pairs, you are asked to consider the following questions. Make notes on your thoughts and feelings about each of them and be prepared to feed back your findings to the larger group.

- What is the difference between empathy and sympathy?
- To what degree is it possible truly to empathize with another person?
- Who can you most easily empathize with?
- With whom would you find empathy difficult?

EMPATHY-BUILDING STATEMENTS

Activity 12

Time required 45 minutes to 1 hour.

Aim of activity To identify some specific empathy-building statements.

Group size Any number between 5 and 25.

Environment A room in which there is space for everyone to sit in a closed circle of chairs and which is large enough for everyone to pair off and spread out, if required. There should be a flipchart and pad or a white/blackboard and marker pens. This is used to jot down comments from group members during discussion periods. Flipchart sheets containing such comments can be pinned to the wall to act as an *aide mémoire*. These can be kept on the wall until the end of the workshop and they help to maintain continuity of content and demonstrate progress.

You may want to present any theoretical points on an acetate sheet, in which case an overhead projector and screen will be required. Any handouts should be prepared prior to using this activity and it is important that there are enough for each person to have one. Reading lists can be given out at the end of the activity and these should be no more than one page long.

Do not hurry people but keep the atmosphere in the group lively and encourage people to share their thoughts and feelings about the activity.

Procedure The large group divides into smaller groups of three or four members. Each group then brainstorms ideas for what would constitute 'empathy-building statements' in counselling. The aim of empathy building is to convey to the client that you, the counsellor, as far as possible understand that person's world-view at present. Empathy-building statements are always tentative and examples of them might include the following:

- *It sounds as though that made you very angry . . .*
- *You seem to be more comfortable now . . .*
- *You seem to be uncertain about that . . .*

Each group tries to identify as many empathy-building statements as possible. After 15 minutes, the group reconvenes and each group, in turn, feeds back their selection. The task of the rest of the group is to decide, as they are read out, whether or not the statements *are* empathy-building. After the group has undertaken this form of peer review, the trainer initiates a more general discussion about the nature, value and limitations of empathy in counselling.

Evaluation Each person in the group makes notes about what they found useful about the activity. Then an evaluative discussion is held with the trainer as facilitator of that discussion.

Closing Participants should be offered a 5-minute period in which to raise questions, express feelings, address particular people in the group or talk through anything else that has arisen from the activity.

PEOPLE WHO EMPATHIZE

Activity 13

Time required 45 minutes to 1 hour.

Aim To explore the qualities of the empathic person.

Group size Any number between 5 and 25.

Environment A room in which there is space for everyone to sit in a closed circle of chairs and which is large enough for everyone to pair off and spread out, if required. There should be a flipchart and pad or a white/blackboard and marker pens. This is used to jot down comments from group members during discussion periods. Flipchart sheets containing such comments can be pinned to the wall to act as an *aide mémoire*. These can be kept on the wall until the end of the workshop and they help to maintain continuity of content and demonstrate progress.

You may want to present any theoretical points on an acetate sheet, in which case an overhead projector and screen will be required. Any handouts should be prepared prior to using this activity and it is important that there are enough for each person to have one. Reading lists can be given out at the end of the activity and these should be no more than one page long.

Keep the activity brisk and the discussion lively. Allow everyone to have their say.

Procedure Each person is given the handout that is reproduced below. Trainees are then asked to complete the table in the handout and to identify nine people that they know and rate them according to the key.

Group members are then invited to pair off and, in those pairs and working with their completed handouts, try to identify what qualities help to make a person appear empathic. After 15 minutes, the group is reconvened and a 'master list' of empathic qualities is drawn up by the trainer from those identified by group members.

If there is time, the items on the list can then be rank-ordered in terms of importance by the group, with the trainer working as the facilitator of this process. Thus the quality that is felt to be most important goes to the top of the list and the quality felt to be least important is put at the bottom. This activity can help to clarify the concept of empathy.

Evaluation The group is divided into pairs and each pair spends 5 minutes discussing what each person liked and disliked about the activity. The group reforms after 5 minutes and an evaluative discussion is held.

Closing Participants should be offered a 5-minute period in which to raise questions, express feelings, address particular people in the group or talk through anything else that has arisen from the activity.

EMPATHY EXERCISE

In the table, below, jot down the names of people who fit the description in the left hand column. In the right hand column, make a note of the degree to which you feel they are empathic.

Person	Name	Empathy rating
A close friend		
A teacher that you liked		
A teacher that you did not like		
A colleague at work		
Someone who fulfils the role of counsellor		
A close member of your family		
A neighbour		
A person you dislike		
You		

Key:

Very empathic	5
Fairly empathic	4
Not very empathic	3
Not at all empathic	2
Don't know	1

SIMPLE REFLECTION OF CONTENT
Activity 14

Time required 45 minutes to 1 hour.

Aim To develop the skill of reflection of content.

Group size Any number between 5 and 25.

Environment A room in which there is space for everyone to sit in a closed circle of chairs and which is large enough for everyone to pair off and spread out, if required. There should be a flipchart and pad or a white/blackboard and marker pens. This is used to jot down comments from group members during discussion periods. Flipchart sheets containing such comments can be pinned to the wall to act as an *aide mémoire*. These can be kept on the wall until the end of the workshop and they help to maintain continuity of content and demonstrate progress.

You may want to present any theoretical points on an acetate sheet, in which case an overhead projector and screen will be required. Any handouts should be prepared prior to using this activity and it is important that there are enough for each person to have one. Reading lists can be given out at the end of the activity and these should be no more than one page long.

Do not hurry people but keep the atmosphere in the group lively and encourage people to share their thoughts and feelings about the activity.

Procedure The group pairs off. One member of each pair acts as 'counsellor' to the other's 'client'. The client talks to the counsellor who uses *only* simple reflection of content as a counselling strategy. Reflection of content involves feeding back the last few words of the client's utterance in order to help them to say more. Here is an example of simple reflection of content in practice:

We lived in Liverpool for a while. We both liked it there although I had some difficulty in settling down.

You had some difficulty in settling down.

Well, it was all new to me. My wife came from that area so she had friends there. The children had no problems, either. They enjoyed going to another school and thought the move was exciting. They all seemed to enjoy it except me.

They all enjoyed it except you.

Don't get me wrong. It wasn't that I didn't like Liverpool. It's just that I find change difficult. After I had been there for six months or so, everything was fine. I suppose, looking back, it wasn't as bad as I'm making it sound. There were some really good things happening around that time as well.

The point about simple reflection is that the counsellor's tone of voice should also echo that of the client. The reflection should not turn into a question, as in the following example.

We lived in Liverpool for a while. We both liked it there although I had some difficulty in settling down.

You had some difficulty in settling down?

Yes.

The point is clear enough. If the reflection turns into a question, then the answer is likely to be short and often monosyllabic. The whole point of reflection here is to encourage the client to develop his train of thought.

After 15 minutes, the pairs swap roles and the new 'counsellors' practise the skill of simple reflection of content. After a further 15 minutes, the larger group reconvenes and the trainer initiates a discussion about the skill and about its limitations. The trainer joins in this activity if there is an odd number of participants.

Evaluation Each person in turn says what they learnt from the activity and what they will take with them back to 'real life', away from the group.

Closing Participants should be offered a 5-minute period in which to raise questions, express feelings, address particular people in the group or talk through anything else that has arisen from the activity.

SIMPLE REFLECTION OF FEELING

Activity 15

Time required 45 minutes to 1 hour.

Aim To practise the skill of reflection of feeling.

Group size Any number between 5 and 25.

Environment A room in which there is space for everyone to sit in a closed circle of chairs and which is large enough for everyone to pair off and spread out, if required. There should be a flipchart and pad or a white/blackboard and marker pens. This is used to jot down comments from group members during discussion periods. Flipchart sheets containing such comments can be pinned to the wall to act as an *aide mémoire*. These can be kept on the wall until the end of the workshop and they help to maintain continuity of content and demonstrate progress.

You may want to present any theoretical points on an acetate sheet, in which case an overhead projector and screen will be required. Any handouts should be prepared prior to using this activity and it is important that there are enough for each person to have one. Reading lists can be given out at the end of the activity and these should be no more than one page long.

Encourage everyone to discuss the activity afterwards and make sure that everyone who wants to say something gets the chance.

Procedure Reflection of feeling differs from reflection of content. In this case, the counsellor attempts to gauge the client's feelings and echoes these back to the client. In many ways, reflection of feeling is similar to the process of building empathy. Here is an example of the reflection of feeling:

I worked in a large office in Fleet Street. It was like a hundred, perhaps a thousand other offices. We all sat there doing what we had to do. It was well paid and I could have worked there for ever, I suppose.

You sound as though you were bored to tears . . .

I was! Looking back, I hated every minute of it. I used to get off the train, get on the bus and push myself to get to the office. I can remember the whole business . . .

You sound angry . . .

I was angry with myself for putting up with it for so long.

For this activity, the group pairs off and each person spends 15 minutes in the role of client to their partner's counsellor. After both parties have practised the skill, the larger group reconvenes and a discussion is developed on the process of reflecting feelings and on the limitations of the process. The trainer takes part in the activity wherever possible.

Evaluation Each person in the group makes notes about what they found useful about the activity. Then an evaluative discussion is held with the trainer as facilitator of that discussion.

Closing Participants should be offered a 5-minute period in which to raise questions, express feelings, address particular people in the group or talk through anything else that has arisen from the activity.

SELECTIVE REFLECTION
Activity 16

Time required 45 minutes to 1 hour.

Aim To develop the skill of selective reflection.

Group size Any number between 5 and 25.

Environment A room in which there is space for everyone to sit in a closed circle of chairs and which is large enough for everyone to pair off and spread out, if required. There should be a flipchart and pad or a white/blackboard and marker pens. This is used to jot down comments from group members during discussion periods. Flipchart sheets containing such comments can be pinned to the wall to act as an *aide mémoire*. These can be kept on the wall until the end of the workshop and they help to maintain continuity of content and demonstrate progress.

You may want to present any theoretical points on an acetate sheet, in which case an overhead projector and screen will be required. Any handouts should be prepared prior to using this activity and it is important that there are enough for each person to have one. Reading lists can be given out at the end of the activity and these should be no more than one page long.

Allow everyone to speak and wait until all thoughts and feelings have been shared in the group before moving on to another activity.

Procedure Selective reflection involves selecting a word or phrase that the client has particularly emphasized. It then involves feeding that word or phrase back to the client as a 'prompt'. Used carefully and skilfully, selective reflection can be a valuable counselling intervention. Here is an example of it:

I wonder sometimes what other people do when it comes to marriage. I suppose a good many people just put up with the way things are. I won't. I don't think it's right to just keep going even when you don't care all that much for each other . . .

You won't just keep going . . .

How can I? We reached the limit a few months ago. We had a big row. I hated it. Still, I suppose everyone rows now and then. You can't expect to go through life without a bit of disagreement.

You hated the row . . .

It was awful. We both said things that we didn't mean. At least, I think we did.

For this activity, the group pairs off and each pair nominates one as counsellor and the other as client. Then, each of the counsellors practises the skill of selective reflection while the client talks. After 15 minutes, roles are reversed and the new clients and counsellors practise the skill. After a further 15 minutes, the larger group reconvenes and everyone feeds back on the activity. A discussion is also held about the process of selective reflection in counselling and on its limitations as a counselling intervention. The trainer takes part in this activity as part of one of the pairs.

Evaluation The group is divided into pairs and each pair spends 5 minutes discussing what each person liked and disliked about the activity. The group reforms after 5 minutes and an evaluative discussion is held.

Closing Participants should be offered a 5-minute period in which to raise questions, express feelings, address particular people in the group or talk through anything else that has arisen from the activity.

PUTTING IT ALL TOGETHER: I

Activity 17

Time required 45 minutes to 1 hour.

Aim To explore a range of counselling interventions.

Group size Any number between 5 and 25.

Environment A room in which there is space for everyone to sit in a closed circle of chairs and which is large enough for everyone to pair off and spread out, if required. There should be a flipchart and pad or a white/blackboard and marker pens. This is used to jot down comments from group members during discussion periods. Flipchart sheets containing such comments can be pinned to the wall to act as an *aide mémoire*. These can be kept on the wall until the end of the workshop and they help to maintain continuity of content and demonstrate progress.

You may want to present any theoretical points on an acetate sheet, in which case an overhead projector and screen will be required. Any handouts should be prepared prior to using this activity and it is important that there are enough for each person to have one. Reading lists can be given out at the end of the activity and these should be no more than one page long.

Keep the activity brisk and the discussion lively. Allow everyone to have their say.

Procedure Each participant is given the handout that follows the details of this activity. The group pairs off and each pair nominates one as counsellor and the other as client. Each counsellor then uses the range of counselling interventions that is listed on the handout but *no others*. The counsellor in each pair initiates the conversation and keeps it going with these interventions. After 20 or 30 minutes roles are reversed and the other halves of the pairs practise their counselling skills, using the handout as a guide.

It is important to emphasize that group members should use only the interventions on the handout as these serve as a basic 'counselling tool-kit'.

After a further 20 or 30 minutes the larger group reconvenes and discusses the activity. The trainer takes part in the activity wherever possible.

Evaluation Each person in turn says what they learnt from the activity and what they will take with them back to 'real life', away from the group.

Closing Participants should be offered a 5-minute period in which to raise questions, express feelings, address particular people in the group or talk through anything else that has arisen from the activity.

EMPATHIC COUNSELLING INTERVENTIONS

These are counselling interventions that tend to convey empathy. Use them during this exercise.

- Simple reflection of feeling
- Simple reflection of content
- Selective reflection
- Summarizing
- Listening

USING EMPATHY IN EVERYDAY LIFE
Activity 18

Time required 45 minutes to 1 hour.

Aim To practise using empathy-building in everyday life.

Group size Any number between 5 and 25.

Environment A room in which there is space for everyone to sit in a closed circle of chairs and which is large enough for everyone to pair off and spread out, if required. There should be a flipchart and pad or a white/blackboard and marker pens. This is used to jot down comments from group members during discussion periods. Flipchart sheets containing such comments can be pinned to the wall to act as an *aide mémoire*. These can be kept on the wall until the end of the workshop and they help to maintain continuity of content and demonstrate progress.

You may want to present any theoretical points on an acetate sheet, in which case an overhead projector and screen will be required. Any handouts should be prepared prior to using this activity and it is important that there are enough for each person to have one. Reading lists can be given out at the end of the activity and these should be no more than one page long.

Allow everyone to speak and wait until all thoughts and feelings have been shared in the group before moving on to another activity.

Procedure Each participant is invited to try using empathy-building skills as soon as possible in everyday life. To enhance this process, they are encouraged to keep a diary in which they record their progress or lack of it. Suggested headings for the diary are as follows:

- Date.
- Locations.
- Examples of empathy-building interventions used.
- Reaction.
- Other comments.
- What I need to do next.

The diary is used as the basis of a discussion, the next time that the group meets. There is no evaluation or closing activity for this exercise.

EMPATHY IN DIFFICULT SITUATIONS

Activity 19

Time required 45 minutes to 1 hour.

Aim To explore the limitations of empathy.

Group size Any number between 5 and 25.

Environment A room in which there is space for everyone to sit in a closed circle of chairs and which is large enough for everyone to pair off and spread out, if required. There should be a flipchart and pad or a white/blackboard and marker pens. This is used to jot down comments from group members during discussion periods. Flipchart sheets containing such comments can be pinned to the wall to act as an *aide mémoire*. These can be kept on the wall until the end of the workshop and they help to maintain continuity of content and demonstrate progress.

You may want to present any theoretical points on an acetate sheet, in which case an overhead projector and screen will be required. Any handouts should be prepared prior to using this activity and it is important that there are enough for each person to have one. Reading lists can be given out at the end of the activity and these should be no more than one page long.

Encourage everyone to discuss the activity afterwards and make sure that everyone who wants to say something gets the chance.

Procedure We cannot all empathize with everyone we meet. All of us are limited, in some way, by our beliefs, values and feelings towards people, behaviour and events. This activity explores some of the limitations of empathy-building.

Each person is given a copy of the handout that accompanies this activity. The trainees discuss in pairs the people that are highlighted in the handout and make notes on what it is about each person that may or may not make empathy difficult.

After 15 minutes, the larger group reconvenes and a discussion is held about the various people in the handout and the group participants' views on empathizing, or otherwise, with each. The final stage of the discussion should focus on what can be done if *you* cannot empathize and should aim at identifying alternative strategies or even alternative agencies.

Evaluation Each person in turn says what they learnt from the activity and what they will take with them back to 'real life', away from the group.

Closing Participants should be offered a 5-minute period in which to raise questions, express feelings, address particular people in the group or talk through anything else that has arisen from the activity.

EMPATHY IN DIFFICULT SITUATIONS

In this exercise, you are asked to consider to what degree you could or could not empathize with the people in this list. Imagine you are counselling each of these people and, as they talk, they tell you about their lives and their background. Try to identify very specifically what might or might not stop you from empathizing.

- A man who has been charged with child abuse.
- A young, unmarried woman who wants to have an abortion.
- A 17-year-old boy who tells you that he is gay.
- A young girl who regularly takes 'ecstasy'.
- A middle-aged man who tells you that he hears 'voices'.
- A woman who tells you that she wants to kill herself.
- A senior colleague who feels he needs to talk to you in confidence about a crisis at home.

ETHICAL ISSUES
Activity 20

Time required 45 minutes to 1 hour.

Aim To explore the ethics of empathy.

Group size Any number between 5 and 25.

Environment A room in which there is space for everyone to sit in a closed circle of chairs and which is large enough for everyone to pair off and spread out, if required. There should be a flipchart and pad or a white/blackboard and marker pens. This is used to jot down comments from group members during discussion periods. Flipchart sheets containing such comments can be pinned to the wall to act as an *aide mémoire*. These can be kept on the wall until the end of the workshop and they help to maintain continuity of content and demonstrate progress.

You may want to present any theoretical points on an acetate sheet, in which case an overhead projector and screen will be required. Any handouts should be prepared prior to using this activity and it is important that there are enough for each person to have one. Reading lists can be given out at the end of the activity and these should be no more than one page long.

Do not hurry people but keep the atmosphere in the group lively and encourage people to share their thoughts and feelings about the activity.

Procedure Counselling is not a panacea. It cannot sort everything out and all counsellors should know their limitations. In this activity, each participant is given the following handout.

The group then divides up into small groups and participants in the small groups discuss the issues on the handouts, making detailed notes as they do so. Particularly, they should address the following issues:

- What are some of the limitations of counselling?
- When should you 'refer on'?
- What are the most difficult aspects of counselling for *you*?

After 15 minutes, the group reconvenes and the trainer develops a discussion on the topics contained in the handout and invites group members to feed back their findings from the smaller group phase of the activity.

Evaluation Each person in the group makes notes about what they found useful about the activity. Then an evaluative discussion is held with the trainer as facilitator of that discussion.

Closing Participants should be offered a 5-minute period in which to raise questions, express feelings, address particular people in the group or talk through anything else that has arisen from the activity.

COUNSELLING ETHICS CHECKLIST

Are you the appropriate person to be counselling?

Is the relationship a *safe* one?

Are you clear about the circumstances in which you would 'refer on'?

As far as you can tell, is your training adequate to cope with this counselling relationship?

Do you have someone *you* can talk to, in confidence, if the need should arise?

Chapter 9:

Information and advice-giving activities

TYPES OF INFORMATION IN COUNSELLING

Activity 21

Time required 45 minutes to 1 hour.

Aim To explore information-giving in counselling.

Group size Any number between 5 and 25.

Environment A room in which there is space for everyone to sit in a closed circle of chairs and which is large enough for everyone to pair off and spread out, if required. There should be a flipchart and pad or a white/blackboard and marker pens. This is used to jot down comments from group members during discussion periods. Flipchart sheets containing such comments can be pinned to the wall to act as an *aide mémoire*. These can be kept on the wall until the end of the workshop and they help to maintain continuity of content and demonstrate progress.

You may want to present any theoretical points on an acetate sheet, in which case an overhead projector and screen will be required. Any handouts should be prepared prior to using this activity and it is important that there are enough for each person to have one. Reading lists can be given out at the end of the activity and these should be no more than one page long.

Keep the activity brisk and the discussion lively. Allow everyone to have their say.

Procedure In earlier chapters of this book, we have noted that, on many occasions, counselling will be a 'client-centred' affair. When it comes to people's life and emotional problems, *they* are usually the experts. There are certain times, however, when it is necessary to be able to give clients clear information.

In this activity, the larger group divides into small ones of about three or four people. Each group then 'brainstorms' all possible situations in which they feel they may be called upon to give information. Here are some examples from groups who have undertaken this activity in the past:

- When the client wants to know what other helping agencies are available.
- When the client wants to know about company policy on a particular issue.
- When a student wants to know about examination procedure.

After 15 minutes, the group reconvenes and the small groups feed back their ideas in the larger. A discussion is facilitated by the trainer about the problems of giving information. The trainer also helps group members to clarify how they intend to stay up to date on the information front.

Evaluation Two 'rounds' are conducted. In the first round, each person in turn says what they liked *least* about the activity. In the second, each person in turn says what they liked *most* about the activity. The trainer joins in this evaluation process and decides whether or not there is a discussion of the points that are raised.

Closing Participants should be offered a 5-minute period in which to raise questions, express feelings, address particular people in the group or talk through anything else that has arisen from the activity.

PROS AND CONS OF ADVICE-GIVING

Activity 22

Time required 45 minutes to 1 hour.

Aim To explore the two sides to information-giving.

Group size Any number between 5 and 25.

Environment A room in which there is space for everyone to sit in a closed circle of chairs and which is large enough for everyone to pair off and spread out, if required. There should be a flipchart and pad or a white/blackboard and marker pens. This is used to jot down comments from group members during discussion periods. Flipchart sheets containing such comments can be pinned to the wall to act as an *aide mémoire*. These can be kept on the wall until the end of the workshop and they help to maintain continuity of content and demonstrate progress.

You may want to present any theoretical points on an acetate sheet, in which case an overhead projector and screen will be required. Any handouts should be prepared prior to using this activity and it is important that there are enough for each person to have one. Reading lists can be given out at the end of the activity and these should be no more than one page long.

Allow everyone to speak and wait until all thoughts and feelings have been shared in the group before moving on to another activity.

Procedure Group participants are given a copy of the handout that accompanies this activity. They are asked to mark it according to their beliefs about the relative values of information-giving in different situations. When everyone has completed the handout, the large group divides into smaller ones for 15 minutes to compare notes. After the 15 minutes, the larger group reconvenes and a discussion is developed about the pros and cons of information-giving. The trainer takes part in this activity as part of one of the smaller groups.

Evaluation Each person in turn says what they learnt from the activity and what they will take with them back to 'real life', away from the group.

Closing Participants should be offered a 5-minute period in which to raise questions, express feelings, address particular people in the group or talk through anything else that has arisen from the activity.

INFORMATION-GIVING EXERCISE

Read through the following counselling situations. In the column next to each item, please place an 'I' if you feel that you *would* give information to the client in this situation. Place an 'N' if you would *not* give information to the client. Consider how you came to these decisions and be prepared to discuss them in small groups. There are no right or wrong answers to this exercise.

	Information?
A girl of 14 asks you about contraceptive practices.	
A student asks you how to plan a research project.	
An 11-year-old asks you what 'safe sex' is.	
A colleague asks you how best to invest money.	
A friend asks you whether or not he should think about getting a divorce.	
A colleague asks you the company policy on smoking.	
A middle-aged man asks if you think that counselling will help him with his psychological problems.	
Your daughter asks you about how best to deal with a bully at school.	

SIMPLE ADVICE-GIVING
Activity 23

Time required 45 minutes to 1 hour.

Aim To explore advice-giving.

Group size Any number between 5 and 25.

Environment A room in which there is space for everyone to sit in a closed circle of chairs and which is large enough for everyone to pair off and spread out, if required. There should be a flipchart and pad or a white/blackboard and marker pens. This is used to jot down comments from group members during discussion periods. Flipchart sheets containing such comments can be pinned to the wall to act as an *aide mémoire*. These can be kept on the wall until the end of the workshop and they help to maintain continuity of content and demonstrate progress.

You may want to present any theoretical points on an acetate sheet, in which case an overhead projector and screen will be required. Any handouts should be prepared prior to using this activity and it is important that there are enough for each person to have one. Reading lists can be given out at the end of the activity and these should be no more than one page long.

Do not hurry people but keep the atmosphere in the group lively and encourage people to share their thoughts and feelings about the activity.

Procedure The group divides into smaller groups of four or five members. In the smaller groups, trainees identify ways in which effective advice-giving should be carried out. They try to identify the personal characteristics of someone who gives advice effectively and also draw up a list of characteristics to avoid. Here is an example of some of the issues that might be uncovered in this activity.

Characteristics of the effective advice-giver
Being clear.
Offering only tentative advice.
Offering only one piece of advice at a time.

Characteristics to avoid
Bossiness.
Arrogance.
Overtalking.

Evaluation Each person in the group makes notes about what they found useful about the activity. Then an evaluative discussion is held with the trainer as facilitator of that discussion.

Closing Participants should be offered a 5-minute period in which to raise questions, express feelings, address particular people in the group or talk through anything else that has arisen from the activity.

GIVING INFORMATION
Activity 24

Time required 45 minutes to 1 hour.

Aim To explore situations in which trainees give advice in their everyday lives.

Group size Any number between 5 and 25.

Environment A room in which there is space for everyone to sit in a closed circle of chairs and which is large enough for everyone to pair off and spread out, if required. There should be a flipchart and pad or a white/blackboard and marker pens. This is used to jot down comments from group members during discussion periods. Flipchart sheets containing such comments can be pinned to the wall to act as an *aide mémoire*. These can be kept on the wall until the end of the workshop and they help to maintain continuity of content and demonstrate progress.

You may want to present any theoretical points on an acetate sheet, in which case an overhead projector and screen will be required. Any handouts should be prepared prior to using this activity and it is important that there are enough for each person to have one. Reading lists can be given out at the end of the activity and these should be no more than one page long.

Keep the activity brisk and the discussion lively. Allow everyone to have their say.

Procedure The group divides into pairs. One of each pair then invites their partner to finish the sentences in the accompanying handout. Respondents are asked to think quickly and to finish the sentences as quickly as possible. When one of the pair has finished the activity, the two swap roles and work through the activity again. After this element has been completed, the larger group reforms and the trainer invokes a discussion about advice-giving in everyday life. The trainer joins in this activity if there is an odd number of participants.

Evaluation The group is divided into pairs and each pair spends 5 minutes discussing what each person liked and disliked about the activity. The group reforms after 5 minutes and an evaluative discussion is held.

Closing Participants should be offered a 5-minute period in which to raise questions, express feelings, address particular people in the group or talk through anything else that has arisen from the activity.

ADVICE-GIVING EXERCISE

In this activity, you are invited to read out the following statements to your partner who is asked to complete the statement. Work fairly quickly through the list and when you have finished, swap roles and work through the list again.

- I often give advice...
- I get given advice by...
- The sort of advice I find most difficult to give is...
- I would never give advice...
- Where advice is concerned, I am the sort of person who...
- The person who always gave me good advice was...
- I react to advice by...
- When other people give me advice, I...
- I never mind being given advice about...
- I would describe myself as...
- The sort of people I avoid are....

BREAKING BAD NEWS
Activity 25

Time required 45 minutes to 1 hour.

Aim To explore the breaking of bad news.

Group size Any number between 5 and 25.

Environment A room in which there is space for everyone to sit in a closed circle of chairs and which is large enough for everyone to pair off and spread out, if required. There should be a flipchart and pad or a white/blackboard and marker pens. This is used to jot down comments from group members during discussion periods. Flipchart sheets containing such comments can be pinned to the wall to act as an *aide mémoire*. These can be kept on the wall until the end of the workshop and they help to maintain continuity of content and demonstrate progress.

You may want to present any theoretical points on an acetate sheet, in which case an overhead projector and screen will be required. Any handouts should be prepared prior to using this activity and it is important that there are enough for each person to have one. Reading lists can be given out at the end of the activity and these should be no more than one page long.

Allow everyone to speak and wait until all thoughts and feelings have been shared in the group before moving on to another activity.

Procedure Many people find breaking bad news difficult. Examples of situations in which bad news must be given include:

- telling someone they have been made redundant;
- telling someone that a close relative has died;
- telling someone that a relationship has ended.

The method of breaking bad news that is practised in this activity is called the 'sandwich method'. It involves the following three elements:

- Warning of the fact that bad news is coming ('Sit down, I have something difficult to talk to you about . . .').
- Breaking the news ('I have to tell you that your job here will end at the beginning of July.').
- Being supportive ('I want us to sit and talk about this . . .').

Various points may be made about this approach. First, the 'warning' element prepares the listener. Second, the bad news itself should be broken directly and in an unambiguous way. There should be no possibility that the hearer will misinterpret the news. Finally, the third layer offers the hearer some support and encouragement following the shock of the news.

In this activity, the group pairs off and practises the use of the sandwich method of breaking bad news. First, one of the pair acts as the bringer of bad news and the other as the listener. Then, after the activity has been run through, the pairs swap roles and the partners practise breaking bad news and hearing it. After a further period of practice, the pair discuss the pros and cons of the method. The handout that accompanies this activity offers topics that may be used by the trainees.

Once both sets of partners have practised the method, the larger group reconvenes and a discussion is invoked about the process of breaking bad news.

Evaluation Two 'rounds' are conducted. In the first round, each person in turn says what they liked *least* about the activity. In the second, each person in turn says what they liked *most* about the activity. The trainer joins in this evaluation process and decides whether or not there is a discussion of the points that are raised.

Closing Participants should be offered a 5-minute period in which to raise questions, express feelings, address particular people in the group or talk through anything else that has arisen from the activity.

BREAKING BAD NEWS

In this activity, you are asked to use the 'sandwich method' of breaking bad news. The three elements of the method are these:

- Say that the bad news is coming
- Disclose the bad news
- Offer support

Use one or more of the following topics for practising the breaking of bad news with this method. Take your time and notice your own and your partner's reaction.

- You are a manager who has to suspend a colleague
- You are a teacher who has to tell a student that he must leave his course
- You are a health care worker who has to tell a mother or father about an accident involving his or her child
- You are a manager who is disciplining a colleague
- You are a lecturer who has to tell a postgraduate student that her research dissertation has failed

CONFRONTATION I
Activity 26

Time required 45 minutes to 1 hour.

Aim To explore confrontation in counselling.

Group size Any number between 5 and 25.

Environment A room in which there is space for everyone to sit in a closed circle of chairs and which is large enough for everyone to pair off and spread out, if required. There should be a flipchart and pad or a white/blackboard and marker pens. This is used to jot down comments from group members during discussion periods. Flipchart sheets containing such comments can be pinned to the wall to act as an *aide mémoire*. These can be kept on the wall until the end of the workshop and they help to maintain continuity of content and demonstrate progress.

You may want to present any theoretical points on an acetate sheet, in which case an overhead projector and screen will be required. Any handouts should be prepared prior to using this activity and it is important that there are enough for each person to have one. Reading lists can be given out at the end of the activity and these should be no more than one page long.

Encourage everyone to discuss the activity afterwards and make sure that everyone who wants to say something gets the chance.

Procedure This activity is simply designed to help people to explore their reaction to being confronted and 'stonewalled' by another person.

The group pairs off. One of each pair is designated 'A' and the other 'B'. 'A' then asks a range of questions of 'B', whose answer is always 'No'. The 'No' can be offered in a variety of tones of voice and with a variety of emphases. After 5 minutes, the pairs swap roles and the 'B's ask questions to which the 'A's respond with 'No's.

After a further 5 minutes, the trainer develops a discussion of the activity and helps the trainees to think about what it is like to be confronted negatively. The trainer takes part in this activity as part of one of the pairs.

Evaluation Each person in turn says what they learnt from the activity and what they will take with them back to 'real life', away from the group.

Closing Participants should be offered a 5-minute period in which to raise questions, express feelings, address particular people in the group or talk through anything else that has arisen from the activity.

CONFRONTATION II
Activity 27

Time required 45 minutes to 1 hour.

Aim To explore *positive* confrontation.

Group size Any number between 5 and 25.

Environment A room in which there is space for everyone to sit in a closed circle of chairs and which is large enough for everyone to pair off and spread out, if required. There should be a flipchart and pad or a white/blackboard and marker pens. This is used to jot down comments from group members during discussion periods. Flipchart sheets containing such comments can be pinned to the wall to act as an *aide mémoire*. These can be kept on the wall until the end of the workshop and they help to maintain continuity of content and demonstrate progress.

You may want to present any theoretical points on an acetate sheet, in which case an overhead projector and screen will be required. Any handouts should be prepared prior to using this activity and it is important that there are enough for each person to have one. Reading lists can be given out at the end of the activity and these should be no more than one page long.

Do not hurry people but keep the atmosphere in the group lively and encourage people to share their thoughts and feelings about the activity.

Procedure This is the reverse of the previous activity and one that can be both hilarious and disturbing by turns. The same format is followed except that the respondents always answer 'Yes' to all the questions – whatever the questions involve. After 5 minutes, roles are reversed and the activity is run through for a further 5 minutes. Trainees are invited to reflect on their response to the activity.

After both partners have worked through the activity, the larger group reconvenes and the trainees are encouraged to discuss the use of both positive and negative confrontation. They can be asked, for example:

- In what situations do you *always* say 'no'?
- In what situations do you *always* say 'yes'?
- Do you ever say 'yes' but *mean* 'no'?
- How is your *real* meaning conveyed?
- How can you be clearer about your positive and negative communication?

The trainer joins in this activity if there is an odd number of participants.

Evaluation Each person in the group makes notes about what they found useful about the activity. Then an evaluative discussion is held with the trainer as facilitator of that discussion.

Closing Participants should be offered a 5-minute period in which to raise questions, express feelings, address particular people in the group or talk through anything else that has arisen from the activity.

GIVING TOO MUCH ADVICE

Activity 28

Time required 45 minutes to 1 hour.

Aim To explore excessive advice-giving.

Group size Any number between 5 and 25.

Environment A room in which there is space for everyone to sit in a closed circle of chairs and which is large enough for everyone to pair off and spread out, if required. There should be a flipchart and pad or a white/blackboard and marker pens. This is used to jot down comments from group members during discussion periods. Flipchart sheets containing such comments can be pinned to the wall to act as an *aide mémoire*. These can be kept on the wall until the end of the workshop and they help to maintain continuity of content and demonstrate progress.

You may want to present any theoretical points on an acetate sheet, in which case an overhead projector and screen will be required. Any handouts should be prepared prior to using this activity and it is important that there are enough for each person to have one. Reading lists can be given out at the end of the activity and these should be no more than one page long.

Encourage everyone to discuss the activity afterwards and make sure that everyone who wants to say something gets the chance.

Procedure Group members pair off and choose one of the topics on the handout. Then, one of each pair acts as counsellor to the other's client. The counsellor then talks to the client for 10 minutes and does almost nothing except offer advice on the topic. The pairs swap roles, and this 'perverse' form of advice-giving is then repeated for a further 10 minutes.

When both parties have adopted the excessive advice-giving role, the larger group reconvenes and a discussion is invoked about appropriate and inappropriate levels of advice giving. The trainer joins in this activity if there is an odd number of participants.

Evaluation Each person in turn says what they learnt from the activity and what they will take with them back to 'real life', away from the group.

Closing Participants should be offered a 5-minute period in which to raise questions, express feelings, address particular people in the group or talk through anything else that has arisen from the activity.

EXCESSIVE ADVICE-GIVING ACTIVITY

You will be invited to pair off. Those of you who are designated 'clients' will adopt one of the following roles. You then tell your 'counsellors' about your situation and they respond. Choose one of these situations to adopt as client:

- You are a student who wonders whether or not they should finish with their boy- or girlfriend
- You are a manager who wonders how they should further their career
- You are a colleague who wants to know how to improve their time-management skills
- You are a student who is experiencing difficulties with their studies
- You are a health-care worker who is worried about the AIDS crisis.

CHECKING FOR UNDERSTANDING
Activity 29

Time required 45 minutes to 1 hour.

Aim To explore the skill of checking for understanding.

Group size Any number between 5 and 25.

Environment A room in which there is space for everyone to sit in a closed circle of chairs and which is large enough for everyone to pair off and spread out, if required. There should be a flipchart and pad or a white/blackboard and marker pens. This is used to jot down comments from group members during discussion periods. Flipchart sheets containing such comments can be pinned to the wall to act as an *aide mémoire*. These can be kept on the wall until the end of the workshop and they help to maintain continuity of content and demonstrate progress.

You may want to present any theoretical points on an acetate sheet, in which case an overhead projector and screen will be required. Any handouts should be prepared prior to using this activity and it is important that there are enough for each person to have one. Reading lists can be given out at the end of the activity and these should be no more than one page long.

Keep the activity brisk and the discussion lively. Allow everyone to have their say.

Procedure The group pairs off. One of each pair acts as client to the other's counsellor. As client, the trainee talks about their current work situation. The aim is to give as full a description of work as possible. Every so often the 'counsellor' checks that they have understood what has been said. Examples of such interventions might include:

- *Let me just check with you . . .*
- *What you seem to be saying is . . .*
- *It sounds as though . . .*
- *Did you say . . .*

The checking for understanding intervention should be used wisely and only when the *content* of what is being said is not clear. The 'counsellors' in this activity have plenty of time to reflect on their *timing* of counselling interventions and should not use the checking-for-understanding approach if it is *not* required. At all times, though, the counsellor should be clear that they really have understood what has been said.

After 10 minutes, roles are reversed for a further 10. When both parties have practised the intervention, the group reconvenes and the trainer invokes a discussion about the pros and cons of checking for understanding in counselling. The trainer takes part in this activity as part of one of the pairs.

Evaluation Two 'rounds' are conducted. In the first round, each person in turn says what they liked *least* about the activity. In the second, each person in turn says what they liked *most* about the activity. The trainer joins in this evaluation process and decides whether or not there is a discussion of the points that are raised.

Closing Participants should be offered a 5-minute period in which to raise questions, express feelings, address particular people in the group or talk through anything else that has arisen from the activity.

INFORMATION-GIVING IN REAL LIFE

Activity 30

Time required 45 minutes to 1 hour.

Aim To explore the use of advice-giving in real life.

Group size Any number between 5 and 25.

Environment A room in which there is space for everyone to sit in a closed circle of chairs and which is large enough for everyone to pair off and spread out, if required. There should be a flipchart and pad or a white/blackboard and marker pens. This is used to jot down comments from group members during discussion periods. Flipchart sheets containing such comments can be pinned to the wall to act as an *aide mémoire*. These can be kept on the wall until the end of the workshop and they help to maintain continuity of content and demonstrate progress.

You may want to present any theoretical points on an acetate sheet, in which case an overhead projector and screen will be required. Any handouts should be prepared prior to using this activity and it is important that there are enough for each person to have one. Reading lists can be given out at the end of the activity and these should be no more than one page long.

Allow everyone to speak and wait until all thoughts and feelings have been shared in the group before moving on to another activity.

Procedure Here, trainees are merely asked to note how they give advice during the coming week. They should be encouraged to reflect on their advice-giving behaviour and to make notes under the following headings:

* Types of advice given.

- Situations in which advice-giving was resisted as an intervention.
- How advice was given.
- Notes for self-improvement.

At the end of the week, or at an agreed time, the trainer invites group members to feed back on the issue of giving advice in everyday life. The trainer takes part in the activity wherever possible.

Evaluation Each person in turn says what they learnt from the activity and what they will take with them back to 'real life', away from the group.

Closing Participants should be offered a 5-minute period in which to raise questions, express feelings, address particular people in the group or talk through anything else that has arisen from the activity.

Chapter 10:

Facilitation activities

EXPLORING FACILITATION

Activity 31

Time required 45 minutes to 1 hour.

Aim To explore the concept of facilitation.

Group size Any number between 5 and 25.

Environment A room in which there is space for everyone to sit in a closed circle of chairs and which is large enough for everyone to pair off and spread out, if required. There should be a flipchart and pad or a white/blackboard and marker pens. This is used to jot down comments from group members during discussion periods. Flipchart sheets containing such comments can be pinned to the wall to act as an *aide mémoire*. These can be kept on the wall until the end of the workshop and they help to maintain continuity of content and demonstrate progress.

You may want to present any theoretical points on an acetate sheet, in which case an overhead projector and screen will be required. Any handouts should be prepared prior to using this activity and it is important that there are enough for each person to have one. Reading lists can be given out at the end of the activity and these should be no more than one page long.

Keep the activity brisk and the discussion lively. Allow everyone to have their say.

Procedure A good deal of counselling is concerned with 'facilitation' or enabling other people. In this activity, the larger group divides up into smaller groups of three or four and 'brainstorms' on the topic of facilitation.

Each group is given a flipchart pad, headed 'Facilitation'. The group elects a spokesman or scribe and the group call out any associations they make with the word. The scribe then jots these down on to the flipchart sheet without any attempt being made at editing what is being offered by group members. After a 10-minute period, the group reconvenes. The flipchart sheets are displayed on the floor in the middle of the group circle and a discussion is generated about the process of facilitation. The trainer draws out what facilitation *is* and what it is *not*.

Evaluation The group is divided into pairs and each pair spends 5 minutes discussing what each person liked and disliked about the activity. The group reforms after 5 minutes and an evaluative discussion is held.

Closing Participants should be offered a 5-minute period in which to raise questions, express feelings, address particular people in the group or talk through anything else that has arisen from the activity.

TYPES OF FACILITATION
Activity 32

Time required 45 minutes to 1 hour.

Aim To explore facilitation styles.

Group size Any number between 5 and 25.

Environment A room in which there is space for everyone to sit in a closed circle of chairs and which is large enough for everyone to pair off and spread out, if required. There should be a flipchart and pad or a white/blackboard and marker pens. This is used to jot down comments from group members during discussion periods. Flipchart sheets containing such comments can be pinned to the wall to act as an *aide mémoire*. These can be kept on the wall until the end of the workshop and they help to maintain continuity of content and demonstrate progress.

You may want to present any theoretical points on an acetate sheet, in which case an overhead projector and screen will be required. Any handouts should be prepared prior to using this activity and it is important that there are enough for each person to have one. Reading lists can be given out at the end of the activity and these should be no more than one page long.

Allow everyone to speak and wait until all thoughts and feelings have been shared in the group before moving on to another activity.

Procedure John Heron (1977) offered an analysis of what he called styles of facilitation. The six dimensions of facilitator style are:

- Directive style
- Informative style
- Confronting style
- Cathartic style

- Catalytic style
- Disclosing style

The person who is directive structures the counselling interview. The person who is informative tends to give lots of information or advice. The confronting counsellor is just that. The cathartic counsellor helps the client to express feelings and the catalytic counsellor is one who 'draws out' the other person. The disclosing counsellor is one who is prepared to share things about themselves with the client. Heron argues that the effective facilitator and counsellor is the one who can use any of the six dimensions of facilitator style effectively.

After an introduction to the six dimensions of facilitator style, trainees are given the following scoresheet and invited to rate themselves in terms of the six. Thus, if they feel they are predominantly cathartic in their counselling, they rate that 6. They rate the next style that they use 5 and so on down to 1. After trainees have rank-ordered the six in this way, the trainer develops a discussion with the group about the nature of the analysis and the importance of flexibility in counselling.

Evaluation Each person in the group makes notes about what they found useful about the activity. Then an evaluative discussion is held with the trainer as facilitator of that discussion.

Closing Participants should be offered a 5-minute period in which to raise questions, express feelings, address particular people in the group or talk through anything else that has arisen from the activity.

DIMENSIONS OF FACILITATOR STYLE

Rank order the following dimensions of facilitator style by placing a figure in the boxes next to the dimensions. Enter a 6 against the style that you use most frequently in your counselling, a 5 in the style that you use next most frequently, down to a 1 for the style that you use least frequently. The dimensions are discussed by John Heron in his 1977 monograph *Dimensions of Facilitator Style*, Human Potential Research Group, University of Surrey, Guildford.

FACILITATOR STYLE	RANK ORDER (1 - 6)
Directive style	
Informative style	
Confronting style	
Cathartic style	
Catalytic style	
Disclosing style	

CLIENT-CENTRED COUNSELLING

Activity 33

Time required 45 minutes to 1 hour.

Aim To explore client-centred counselling.

Group size Any number between 5 and 25.

Environment A room in which there is space for everyone to sit in a closed circle of chairs and which is large enough for everyone to pair off and spread out, if required. There should be a flipchart and pad or a white/blackboard and marker pens. This is used to jot down comments from group members during discussion periods. Flipchart sheets containing such comments can be pinned to the wall to act as an *aide mémoire*. These can be kept on the wall until the end of the workshop and they help to maintain continuity of content and demonstrate progress.

You may want to present any theoretical points on an acetate sheet, in which case an overhead projector and screen will be required. Any handouts should be prepared prior to using this activity and it is important that there are enough for each person to have one. Reading lists can be given out at the end of the activity and these should be no more than one page long.

Encourage everyone to discuss the activity afterwards and make sure that everyone who wants to say something gets the chance.

Procedure Client-centred counselling was developed by Carl Rogers (1952, 1967). It depends on the counsellor allowing the client to make their own decisions in the counselling relationship. The approach is discussed in Chapter 1.

After a short theory input on the client-centred approach by the trainer, the group divides into small groups to discuss the pros and cons of the client-centred approach as it applies to their own work situation. After 15 minutes, the larger group is reconvened and a discussion is held focusing on the positive and negative aspects of client-centred counselling and how its principles may be applied in a range of work situations. Group members may also be encouraged to identify the following:

- The qualities of a client-centred counsellor.
- The skills needed to work as a client-centred counsellor.

Evaluation Two 'rounds' are conducted. In the first round, each person in turn says what they liked *least* about the activity. In the second, each person in turn says what they liked *most* about the activity. The trainer joins in this evaluation process and decides whether or not there is a discussion of the points that are raised.

Closing Participants should be offered a 5-minute period in which to raise questions, express feelings, address particular people in the group or talk through anything else that has arisen from the activity.

LEARNING TO FACILITATE
Activity 34

Time required 45 minutes to 1 hour.

Aim To explore the process of learning to be facilitative.

Group size Any number between 5 and 25.

Environment A room in which there is space for everyone to sit in a closed circle of chairs and which is large enough for everyone to pair off and spread out, if required. There should be a flipchart and pad or a white/blackboard and marker pens. This is used to jot down comments from group members during discussion periods. Flipchart sheets containing such comments can be pinned to the wall to act as an *aide mémoire*. These can be kept on the wall until the end of the workshop and they help to maintain continuity of content and demonstrate progress.

You may want to present any theoretical points on an acetate sheet, in which case an overhead projector and screen will be required. Any handouts should be prepared prior to using this activity and it is important that there are enough for each person to have one. Reading lists can be given out at the end of the activity and these should be no more than one page long.

Do not hurry people but keep the atmosphere in the group lively and encourage people to share their thoughts and feelings about the activity.

Procedure The group members pair off. In pairs, they then explore the question 'How did you learn to be facilitative?'

The question can be explored from a variety of angles:

- The effects of childhood experience.

- Formal training and education.
- Workshops and training courses.
- Management courses.
- Work experience.
- Everyday life.
- Family life.

The aim is for one person in each pair to ask the question of the other. The other person then answers the question as fully as possible while the questioner listens to the answer. After 10 minutes, roles are reversed, the listener becoming the questioner and vice versa. After a further 10 minutes, the larger group reconvenes and a discussion is invoked on how facilitation is or is not learned.

Evaluation Each person in turn says what they learnt from the activity and what they will take with them back to 'real life', away from the group.

Closing Participants should be offered a 5-minute period in which to raise questions, express feelings, address particular people in the group or talk through anything else that has arisen from the activity.

GROUP FACILITATION
Activity 35

Time required 45 minutes to 1 hour.

Aim To experiment with group facilitation.

Group size Any number between 5 and 25.

Environment A room in which there is space for everyone to sit in a closed circle of chairs and which is large enough for everyone to pair off and spread out, if required. There should be a flipchart and pad or a white/blackboard and marker pens. This is used to jot down comments from group members during discussion periods. Flipchart sheets containing such comments can be pinned to the wall to act as an *aide mémoire*. These can be kept on the wall until the end of the workshop and they help to maintain continuity of content and demonstrate progress.

You may want to present any theoretical points on an acetate sheet, in which case an overhead projector and screen will be required. Any handouts should be prepared prior to using this activity and it is important that there are enough for each person to have one. Reading lists can be given out at the end of the activity and these should be no more than one page long.

Encourage everyone to discuss the activity afterwards and make sure that everyone who wants to say something gets the chance.

Procedure The facilitative approach can be developed in a group context. It can also be *used* in the process of running a group discussion. In this activity, one or two people are asked to volunteer to run a group discussion, on any topic they choose. They then facilitate the discussion by using *ONLY* the following group interventions:

● Open questions.

- Checking for understanding.
- Empathy building.
- Reflection.

These interventions are used for a period of about half an hour. After that period, the person or pair stops using the interventions and is offered feedback on their skill (or relative lack of it) by the rest of the group. The trainer then develops a discussion with the group on the process of group facilitation and how group members might use it in their work situations. The trainer joins in this activity wherever possible.

Evaluation The group is divided into pairs and each pair spends 5 minutes discussing what each person liked and disliked about the activity. The group reforms after 5 minutes and an evaluative discussion is held.

Closing Participants should be offered a 5-minute period in which to raise questions, express feelings, address particular people in the group or talk through anything else that has arisen from the activity.

ON THE RECEIVING END
Activity 36

Time required 45 minutes to 1 hour.

Aim To explore what it is like to be 'facilitated'.

Group size Any number between 5 and 25.

Environment A room in which there is space for everyone to sit in a closed circle of chairs and which is large enough for everyone to pair off and spread out, if required. There should be a flipchart and pad or a white/blackboard and marker pens. This is used to jot down comments from group members during discussion periods. Flipchart sheets containing such comments can be pinned to the wall to act as an *aide mémoire*. These can be kept on the wall until the end of the workshop and they help to maintain continuity of content and demonstrate progress.

You may want to present any theoretical points on an acetate sheet, in which case an overhead projector and screen will be required. Any handouts should be prepared prior to using this activity and it is important that there are enough for each person to have one. Reading lists can be given out at the end of the activity and these should be no more than one page long.

Allow everyone to speak and wait until all thoughts and feelings have been shared in the group before moving on to another activity.

Procedure The group pairs off. In each pair, one is nominated the 'counsellor' and the other the 'client'. The 'counsellors' then use facilitative interventions of the sort described in the previous activity to encourage their clients to talk. After 10 minutes, the 'clients' all report back to their counsellors on their relative skill levels in using facilitative interventions. The aim of this evaluative period is *only* to evaluate the counsellors' skill in being facilitative.

After a further 5 minutes, roles are swapped; the clients become counsellors and *their* skills are evaluated for a 5-minute period.

The larger group reconvenes and the pairs feed back about their experiences to the group. Accent is placed on the 'counsellors' talking about their own skill levels and on 'clients' talking about what it was like to be on the receiving end of facilitative counselling. This is a useful activity for highlighting the relative pros and cons of facilitative counselling and the client-centred approach in general. The trainer takes part in the activity wherever possible.

Evaluation Each person in the group makes notes about what they found useful about the activity. Then an evaluative discussion is held with the trainer as facilitator of that discussion.

Closing Participants should be offered a 5-minute period in which to raise questions, express feelings, address particular people in the group or talk through anything else that has arisen from the activity.

LIMITS TO FACILITATION
Activity 37

Time required 45 minutes to 1 hour.

Aim To explore situations in which the facilitative approach may not be appropriate.

Group size Any number between 5 and 25.

Environment A room in which there is space for everyone to sit in a closed circle of chairs and which is large enough for everyone to pair off and spread out, if required. There should be a flipchart and pad or a white/blackboard and marker pens. This is used to jot down comments from group members during discussion periods. Flipchart sheets containing such comments can be pinned to the wall to act as an *aide mémoire*. These can be kept on the wall until the end of the workshop and they help to maintain continuity of content and demonstrate progress.

You may want to present any theoretical points on an acetate sheet, in which case an overhead projector and screen will be required. Any handouts should be prepared prior to using this activity and it is important that there are enough for each person to have one. Reading lists can be given out at the end of the activity and these should be no more than one page long.

Keep the activity brisk and the discussion lively. Allow everyone to have their say.

Procedure The group divides into smaller groups of four or five. Trainees then identify situations in which being facilitative would *not* be the appropriate approach to counselling. Particularly, they are asked to reflect on work-related situations and this activity is particularly useful in a multi-disciplinary workshop.

After 10 minutes, each group is given a flipchart sheet and a pen.

Each group elects a scribe who writes a summary of what was discussed in their group. After a further 5 minutes, the larger group reconvenes and the flipchart sheets are placed on the floor in the centre of the group to enable all members to review them. The trainer then invokes a discussion of the situations in which the facilitative approach may not be best. In each situation that arises, group members are invited to play 'devil's advocate'. If they feel that in any particular situation the facilitative approach *could* be used, they are asked to say so and to illustrate how this might be the case. The trainer takes part in the activity wherever possible.

Evaluation Each person in turn says what they learnt from the activity and what they will take with them back to 'real life', away from the group.

Closing Participants should be offered a 5-minute period in which to raise questions, express feelings, address particular people in the group or talk through anything else that has arisen from the activity.

BECOMING AN EFFECTIVE COUNSELLOR
Activity 38

Time required 45 minutes to 1 hour.

Aim To identify group members' new aims as counsellors.

Group size Any number between 5 and 25.

Environment A room in which there is space for everyone to sit in a closed circle of chairs and which is large enough for everyone to pair off and spread out, if required. There should be a flipchart and pad or a white/blackboard and marker pens. This is used to jot down comments from group members during discussion periods. Flipchart sheets containing such comments can be pinned to the wall to act as an *aide mémoire*. These can be kept on the wall until the end of the workshop and they help to maintain continuity of content and demonstrate progress.

You may want to present any theoretical points on an acetate sheet, in which case an overhead projector and screen will be required. Any handouts should be prepared prior to using this activity and it is important that there are enough for each person to have one. Reading lists can be given out at the end of the activity and these should be no more than one page long.

Allow everyone to speak and wait until all thoughts and feelings have been shared in the group before moving on to another activity.

Procedure The group divides into pairs. One of each pair asks their partner the following question *three* times and listens to the answer in each case:

What do you need to do now to become a more effective counsellor?

Each time the question is asked, the colleague is allowed to explore it in more detail. After each 'talker' has answered the question three times, roles are reversed and the partner explores the question three times.

When all participants have answered the question three times, the larger group reconvenes and a discussion is held about what group members need to do to become more effective as counsellors. These issues are written on to a flipchart sheet or a black- or whiteboard by the trainer and participants are encouraged to develop personal aims or goals. The trainer takes part in this activity as part of one of the pairs.

Evaluation The group is divided into pairs and each pair spends 5 minutes discussing what each person liked and disliked about the activity. The group reforms after 5 minutes and an evaluative discussion is held.

Closing Participants should be offered a 5-minute period in which to raise questions, express feelings, address particular people in the group or talk through anything else that has arisen from the activity.

PUTTING IT ALL TOGETHER: II
Activity 39

Time required 1-1½ hours.

Aim To consolidate learning.

Group size Any number between 5 and 25.

Environment A room in which there is space for everyone to sit in a closed circle of chairs and which is large enough for everyone to pair off and spread out, if required. There should be a flipchart and pad or a white/blackboard and marker pens. This is used to jot down comments from group members during discussion periods. Flipchart sheets containing such comments can be pinned to the wall to act as an *aide mémoire*. These can be kept on the wall until the end of the workshop and they help to maintain continuity of content and demonstrate progress.

You may want to present any theoretical points on an acetate sheet, in which case an overhead projector and screen will be required. Any handouts should be prepared prior to using this activity and it is important that there are enough for each person to have one. Reading lists can be given out at the end of the activity and these should be no more than one page long.

Encourage everyone to discuss the activity afterwards and make sure that everyone who wants to say something gets the chance.

Procedure The group members pair off and each pair nominates one as counsellor and one as client. The counsellor then spends half an hour in the role of facilitative counsellor, encouraging the client to talk and to discuss anything that comes up. The aim is for the counsellor to 'follow' the client and to enable the client to talk about topics of his or her own choice. After half an hour roles are reversed after a short break and the counsellors become clients.

After a further half an hour, the larger group reconvenes and the trainer encourages the trainees to discuss the activity and to highlight their own strengths and deficits in facilitative counselling. The trainer joins in this activity if there is an odd number of participants.

Evaluation Two 'rounds' are conducted. In the first round, each person in turn says what they liked *least* about the activity. In the second, each person in turn says what they liked *most* about the activity. The trainer joins in this evaluation process and decides whether or not there is a discussion of the points that are raised.

Closing Participants should be offered a 5-minute period in which to raise questions, express feelings, address particular people in the group or talk through anything else that has arisen from the activity.

DEALING WITH CONTINGENCIES

Activity 40

Time required 45 minutes to 1 hour.

Aim To identify strategies for coping in difficult situations.

Group size Any number between 5 and 25.

Environment A room in which there is space for everyone to sit in a closed circle of chairs and which is large enough for everyone to pair off and spread out, if required. There should be a flipchart and pad or a white/blackboard and marker pens. This is used to jot down comments from group members during discussion periods. Flipchart sheets containing such comments can be pinned to the wall to act as an *aide mémoire*. These can be kept on the wall until the end of the workshop and they help to maintain continuity of content and demonstrate progress.

You may want to present any theoretical points on an acetate sheet, in which case an overhead projector and screen will be required. Any handouts should be prepared prior to using this activity and it is important that there are enough for each person to have one. Reading lists can be given out at the end of the activity and these should be no more than one page long.

Do not hurry people but keep the atmosphere in the group lively and encourage people to share their thoughts and feelings about the activity.

Procedure Facilitative counselling can encourage considerable disclosure on the part of the client. Sometimes, 'difficult' disclosures are made. This exercise encourages group members to explore strategies for coping with such disclosures.

The group divides into smaller groups of four or five. Each group member is given the handout that follows this activity. They are then asked to explore what each of them would do if the disclosures on the handout where made to *them*. As much diversity of response as possible is encouraged and one member of each group takes notes of the discussion that takes place.

After half an hour, the larger group reconvenes and the trainer leads a discussion on how those contingencies may be handled, emphasizing that there are no 'correct' responses. Everyone in the group is allowed a hearing. The trainer takes part in the activity wherever possible.

Evaluation Each person in turn says what they learnt from the activity and what they will take with them back to 'real life', away from the group.

Closing Participants should be offered a 5-minute period in which to raise questions, express feelings, address particular people in the group or talk through anything else that has arisen from the activity.

DIFFICULT SITUATIONS

How would YOU deal with the following disclosures if they were made to you in a counselling relationship?

- A young colleague tells you that she is pregnant and that she cannot tell anyone else
- A young colleague tells you that he is gay
- A middle-aged, opposite-sex colleague tells you that they are in love with you
- A young colleague reports being harassed by one of your seniors
- A senior member of staff tells you they have committed a crime
- A senior member of staff starts to cry while talking to you

Chapter 11:

Problem-solving activities

TYPES OF PROBLEM
Activity 41

Time required 45 minutes to 1 hour.

Aim To explore the sort of problem that trainees encounter in counselling.

Group size Any number between 5 and 25.

Environment A room in which there is space for everyone to sit in a closed circle of chairs and which is large enough for everyone to pair off and spread out, if required. There should be a flipchart and pad or a white/blackboard and marker pens. This is used to jot down comments from group members during discussion periods. Flipchart sheets containing such comments can be pinned to the wall to act as an *aide mémoire*. These can be kept on the wall until the end of the workshop and they help to maintain continuity of content and demonstrate progress.

You may want to present any theoretical points on an acetate sheet, in which case an overhead projector and screen will be required. Any handouts should be prepared prior to using this activity and it is important that there are enough for each person to have one. Reading lists can be given out at the end of the activity and these should be no more than one page long.

Keep the activity brisk and the discussion lively. Allow everyone to have their say.

Procedure As we have noted earlier, there are different sorts of counselling. There are also different sorts of problem. The aim of this activity is to encourage trainees to identify their points of similarity and difference.

The group divides into smaller groups. Each sub-group elects a scribe who jots down the thoughts of all group members on to a flipchart pad. Each group is asked to brainstorm 'the sort of problem that your clients bring to you in counselling'. The aim here is to identify as many different sorts of problem as possible. Examples of the sort of problem that may arise in this activity are as follows:

- Students with exam-related problems.
- Family difficulties.
- Worries about careers.
- Sexual problems.
- Relationship difficulties.
- Money worries.

The small groups brainstorm for about 15 minutes and then the larger group reconvenes. All the flipchart sheets are then pinned to the wall and all group members are invited to view them and to place a tick against two problems that they commonly encounter.

The trainer then encourages a discussion of some of the more common difficulties and explores with the group the less-commonly encountered problems. He may also want to explore with the group Carl Rogers' (1967) assertion that 'that which is most personal is most general'. (The things that you and I worry about are also the things that *most* people worry about, according to Rogers.)

Evaluation Each person in the group makes notes about what they found useful about the activity. Then an evaluative discussion is held with the trainer as facilitator of that discussion.

Closing Participants should be offered a 5-minute period in which to raise questions, express feelings, address particular people in the group or talk through anything else that has arisen from the activity.

IDENTIFYING PROBLEMS
Activity 42

Time required 45 minutes to 1 hour.

Aim To explore ways of helping clients to identify problems.

Group size Any number between 5 and 25.

Environment A room in which there is space for everyone to sit in a closed circle of chairs and which is large enough for everyone to pair off and spread out, if required. There should be a flipchart and pad or a white/blackboard and marker pens. This is used to jot down comments from group members during discussion periods. Flipchart sheets containing such comments can be pinned to the wall to act as an *aide mémoire*. These can be kept on the wall until the end of the workshop and they help to maintain continuity of content and demonstrate progress.

You may want to present any theoretical points on an acetate sheet, in which case an overhead projector and screen will be required. Any handouts should be prepared prior to using this activity and it is important that there are enough for each person to have one. Reading lists can be given out at the end of the activity and these should be no more than one page long.

Allow everyone to speak and wait until all thoughts and feelings have been shared in the group before moving on to another activity.

Procedure The group pairs off. One of each pair is nominated 'A' and the other 'B'. The 'B's listen while the 'A's identify how they help their clients to identify problems. Some of the methods that have be identified by other people who have done this exercise are:

- By direct questions.
- By the counsellor self-disclosing their own problems.
- By listening to the client.

- By encouraging the client to talk.
- By helping to focus the client's discussion.

After 10 minutes, roles are reversed. The 'A's then listen to the 'B's as *they* identify how they help their clients to identify problems. After a further 10 minutes, the trainer encourages the larger group to reform and facilitates a discussion on problem identification. The trainer takes part in this activity as part of one of the pairs.

Evaluation Two 'rounds' are conducted. In the first round, each person in turn says what they liked *least* about the activity. In the second, each person in turn says what they liked *most* about the activity. The trainer joins in this evaluation process and decides whether or not there is a discussion of the points that are raised.

Closing Participants should be offered a 5-minute period in which to raise questions, express feelings, address particular people in the group or talk through anything else that has arisen from the activity.

A PROBLEM-SOLVING CYCLE

Activity 43

Time required 45 minutes to 1 hour.

Aim To explore a problem-solving cycle.

Group size Any number between 5 and 25.

Environment A room in which there is space for everyone to sit in a closed circle of chairs and which is large enough for everyone to pair off and spread out, if required. There should be a flipchart and pad or a white/blackboard and marker pens. This is used to jot down comments from group members during discussion periods. Flipchart sheets containing such comments can be pinned to the wall to act as an *aide mémoire*. These can be kept on the wall until the end of the workshop and they help to maintain continuity of content and demonstrate progress.

You may want to present any theoretical points on an acetate sheet, in which case an overhead projector and screen will be required. Any handouts should be prepared prior to using this activity and it is important that there are enough for each person to have one. Reading lists can be given out at the end of the activity and these should be no more than one page long.

Encourage everyone to discuss the activity afterwards and make sure that everyone who wants to say something gets the chance.

Procedure The trainer develops a discussion following the previous activity on the question 'How do we help people to solve problems?' and encourages the group to identify a definite *method* of problem-solving. If possible, the trainer builds up a problem-solving cycle – a means of working through problems. If such a cycle is not developed by the group, they are offered the following handout.

After the trainees have identified a problem-solving cycle or when the trainer has discussed the above cycle, the whole group discusses the pros and cons of using such a cycle in everyday counselling.

Evaluation Each person in turn says what they learnt from the activity and what they will take with them back to 'real life', away from the group.

Closing Participants should be offered a 5-minute period in which to raise questions, express feelings, address particular people in the group or talk through anything else that has arisen from the activity.

PROBLEM-SOLVING CYCLE

Stage one	Clarification of problem: The counsellor and client discuss the problem until BOTH are clear about its nature.
Stage two	Generation of possible solutions. The counsellor and client 'brainstorm' all possible solutions.
Stage three	Choice of solution. The client identifies the preferred solution.
Stage four	Practice. The client tries the solution to the problem.
Stage five	Evaluation. The client and counsellor explore how effective or otherwise the strategy was. If it was *not* effective, they return to stages one and two, restate the problem and generate other solutions.

CLARIFYING PROBLEMS
Activity 44

Time required 45 minutes to 1 hour.

Aim To explore the clarification of clients' problems.

Group size Any number between 5 and 25.

Environment A room in which there is space for everyone to sit in a closed circle of chairs and which is large enough for everyone to pair off and spread out, if required. There should be a flipchart and pad or a white/blackboard and marker pens. This is used to jot down comments from group members during discussion periods. Flipchart sheets containing such comments can be pinned to the wall to act as an *aide mémoire*. These can be kept on the wall until the end of the workshop and they help to maintain continuity of content and demonstrate progress.

You may want to present any theoretical points on an acetate sheet, in which case an overhead projector and screen will be required. Any handouts should be prepared prior to using this activity and it is important that there are enough for each person to have one. Reading lists can be given out at the end of the activity and these should be no more than one page long.

Do not hurry people but keep the atmosphere in the group lively and encourage people to share their thoughts and feelings about the activity.

Procedure The first stage of the cycle in the previous activity was the clarification of the problem. Often in counselling, solutions are not forthcoming because the problem has not been clarified sufficiently.

The group pairs off. One of each pair leads a discussion in which their partner talks through a work-related or home-related problem. The following strategies can be used in this discussion:

- The listener encourages the talker to give a general description of the problem area.
- The listener then suggests that the talker tries to summarize the problem *in one sentence*.
- The listener then asks if there are *related* problems.

By working through these stages, the pair can clarify a particular problem and reduce it to a manageable issue. Not all life situations can be reduced in this way but many personal and emotional problems *can* be.

After 10 minutes, roles are reversed; the 'listener' becomes the 'explorer' in each pair and they work through the above stages. After a further 10 minutes, the larger group reconvenes and the trainer facilitates a discussion about the clarification of problems, paying particular attention to the following issues:

- Encouraging the client to talk about the *background* to the problem.
- Facilitating the expression of a problem in a *single sentence*.
- Helping the client to identify future *aims*.
- Discussing problem-solving *strategies* with clients.
- Evaluating problem-solving.

Evaluation The group is divided into pairs and each pair spends 5 minutes discussing what each person liked and disliked about the activity. The group reforms after 5 minutes and an evaluative discussion is held.

Closing Participants should be offered a 5-minute period in which to raise questions, express feelings, address particular people in the group or talk through anything else that has arisen from the activity.

HOW *YOU* DEAL WITH PROBLEMS

Activity 45

Time required 45 minutes to 1 hour.

Aim To identify how trainees deal with their own problems.

Group size Any number between 5 and 25.

Environment A room in which there is space for everyone to sit in a closed circle of chairs and which is large enough for everyone to pair off and spread out, if required. There should be a flipchart and pad or a white/blackboard and marker pens. This is used to jot down comments from group members during discussion periods. Flipchart sheets containing such comments can be pinned to the wall to act as an *aide mémoire*. These can be kept on the wall until the end of the workshop and they help to maintain continuity of content and demonstrate progress.

You may want to present any theoretical points on an acetate sheet, in which case an overhead projector and screen will be required. Any handouts should be prepared prior to using this activity and it is important that there are enough for each person to have one. Reading lists can be given out at the end of the activity and these should be no more than one page long.

Encourage everyone to discuss the activity afterwards and make sure that everyone who wants to say something gets the chance.

Procedure To help others sort out their problems, we must be at least minimally skilled in identifying and solving some of our own. Not to be able to would be hypocritical.

The group pairs off. One of each pair then asks the following question of their partner three times during the course of a 10-minute period:

How do you solve your own *problems?*

Each time the question is asked, the trainee is encouraged to explore the question in greater depth. After 10 minutes, roles are reversed and partners again work through the thrice-asked question. After a further 10 minutes, the facilitator encourages group members to feed back their findings from the activity.

Evaluation Two 'rounds' are conducted. In the first round, each person in turn says what they liked *least* about the activity. In the second, each person in turn says what they liked *most* about the activity. The trainer joins in this evaluation process and decides whether or not there is a discussion of the points that are raised.

Closing Participants should be offered a 5-minute period in which to raise questions, express feelings, address particular people in the group or talk through anything else that has arisen from the activity.

LIMITATIONS OF ADVICE-GIVING

Activity 46

Time required 45 minutes to 1 hour.

Aim To explore strategies *other* than giving advice.

Group size Any number between 5 and 25.

Environment A room in which there is space for everyone to sit in a closed circle of chairs and which is large enough for everyone to pair off and spread out, if required. There should be a flipchart and pad or a white/blackboard and marker pens. This is used to jot down comments from group members during discussion periods. Flipchart sheets containing such comments can be pinned to the wall to act as an *aide mémoire*. These can be kept on the wall until the end of the workshop and they help to maintain continuity of content and demonstrate progress.

You may want to present any theoretical points on an acetate sheet, in which case an overhead projector and screen will be required. Any handouts should be prepared prior to using this activity and it is important that there are enough for each person to have one. Reading lists can be given out at the end of the activity and these should be no more than one page long.

Allow everyone to speak and wait until all thoughts and feelings have been shared in the group before moving on to another activity.

Procedure The trainer invites the group to pair off and to consider the scenarios that are described on the handout that accompanies this activity. They are then asked to discuss, in their pairs, counselling strategies *other than* advice-giving that could be used in helping the people concerned. The pairs are asked to identify as many strategies as possible.

After 10 or 15 minutes the larger group reconvenes and the trainer encourages a discussion of alternative counselling strategies. The trainer takes part in this activity as part of one of the pairs.

Evaluation Each person in turn says what they learnt from the activity and what they will take with them back to 'real life', away from the group.

Closing Participants should be offered a 5-minute period in which to raise questions, express feelings, address particular people in the group or talk through anything else that has arisen from the activity.

COUNSELLING STRATEGIES

Read through the following scenarios and identify *as specifically as you can* as many counselling strategies *other than advice-giving* that could be used to help the people concerned. There are no right answers – try to think as broadly and as deeply as possible about the sort of helping strategies you might use.

- A younger colleague asks your advice about buying a house for the first time. He is about to be married and is nervous about the financial implications of his purchase.
- A colleague of equal status to you asks to talk to you about her marriage. She discloses to you that she believes that her husband is having an affair with another man.
- A senior colleague complains of being depressed and finds that he can talk to you. He sits quietly with you and doesn't say very much but does say that he appreciates the chance to share his feelings with you.

WORKING OUT A PLAN
Activity 47

Time required 45 minutes to 1 hour.

Aim To identify the planning stages of problem-solving.

Group size Any number between 5 and 25.

Environment A room in which there is space for everyone to sit in a closed circle of chairs and which is large enough for everyone to pair off and spread out, if required. There should be a flipchart and pad or a white/blackboard and marker pens. This is used to jot down comments from group members during discussion periods. Flipchart sheets containing such comments can be pinned to the wall to act as an *aide mémoire*. These can be kept on the wall until the end of the workshop and they help to maintain continuity of content and demonstrate progress.

You may want to present any theoretical points on an acetate sheet, in which case an overhead projector and screen will be required. Any handouts should be prepared prior to using this activity and it is important that there are enough for each person to have one. Reading lists can be given out at the end of the activity and these should be no more than one page long.

Keep the activity brisk and the discussion lively. Allow everyone to have their say.

Procedure Part of problem-solving is the development of a plan of action. The elements of this are:

- the clarification of the problem;
- the identification of a solution;
- the drawing up of aims or goals.

For this activity, the group divides into small sub-groups of four or five. Each of the smaller groups discusses the skills needed by a counsellor in helping clients to develop a problem-solving plan. They should also identify the difficulties associated with such planning. Before they return to the larger group, they should be clear about the following things:

- how they would help to clarify problems;
- how they would help the client to identify a solution;
- how they would draw up aims or goals. Of particular importance here is the need for an aim or goal to describe only *one* behaviour or element of change.

After 15 minutes, the larger group reconvenes. The trainer initiates a feedback session in which all sub-group members are invited to discuss their findings.

Evaluation The group is divided into pairs and each pair spends 5 minutes discussing what each person liked and disliked about the activity. The group reforms after 5 minutes and an evaluative discussion is held.

Closing Participants should be offered a 5-minute period in which to raise questions, express feelings, address particular people in the group or talk through anything else that has arisen from the activity.

IMPLEMENTING THE PLAN

Activity 48

Time required 45 minutes to 1 hour.

Aim To identify the role of the counsellor when the client is implementing a problem-solving plan.

Group size Any number between 5 and 25.

Environment A room in which there is space for everyone to sit in a closed circle of chairs and which is large enough for everyone to pair off and spread out, if required. There should be a flipchart and pad or a white/blackboard and marker pens. This is used to jot down comments from group members during discussion periods. Flipchart sheets containing such comments can be pinned to the wall to act as an *aide mémoire*. These can be kept on the wall until the end of the workshop and they help to maintain continuity of content and demonstrate progress.

You may want to present any theoretical points on an acetate sheet, in which case an overhead projector and screen will be required. Any handouts should be prepared prior to using this activity and it is important that there are enough for each person to have one. Reading lists can be given out at the end of the activity and these should be no more than one page long.

Do not hurry people but keep the atmosphere in the group lively and encourage people to share their thoughts and feelings about the activity.

Procedure The action that occurs when problem-solving strategies are being implemented often takes place away from the counsellor/client relationship. The counsellor's role was that of helper in the development of the plan. It is the client who has to implement it and the client who has to change.

The group pairs off and each of the pairs discusses the following question:

What is the role of the counsellor during the implementation of a problem-solving plan?

Particular attention should be paid to the following issues:

- Keeping a low profile.
- Avoiding excess 'fathering' or 'mothering'.
- Being supportive.
- Being available.
- Responding to change.

After a 10-minute period in pairs, the larger group reconvenes. The trainer develops a discussion about the supportive role of the counsellor in the counselling relationships and may also encourage discussion about ending the client/counsellor relationship and the problems that can arise during this delicate stage. Particular attention here should be paid to the following issues:

- Ways of ending the relationship.
- Who ends it?
- How to say 'goodbye'.
- Should you stay in touch?
- Separation.
- Dependence.

Evaluation Two 'rounds' are conducted. In the first round, each person in turn says what they liked *least* about the activity. In the second, each person in turn says what they liked *most* about the activity. The trainer joins in this evaluation process and decides whether or not there is a discussion of the points that are raised.

Closing Participants should be offered a 5-minute period in which to raise questions, express feelings, address particular people in the group or talk through anything else that has arisen from the activity.

EVALUATING THE PROBLEM-SOLVING

Activity 49

Time required 45 minutes to 1 hour.

Aim To explore evaluation of the problem-solving process.

Group size Any number between 5 and 25.

Environment A room in which there is space for everyone to sit in a closed circle of chairs and which is large enough for everyone to pair off and spread out, if required. There should be a flipchart and pad or a white/blackboard and marker pens. This is used to jot down comments from group members during discussion periods. Flipchart sheets containing such comments can be pinned to the wall to act as an *aide mémoire*. These can be kept on the wall until the end of the workshop and they help to maintain continuity of content and demonstrate progress.

You may want to present any theoretical points on an acetate sheet, in which case an overhead projector and screen will be required. Any handouts should be prepared prior to using this activity and it is important that there are enough for each person to have one. Reading lists can be given out at the end of the activity and these should be no more than one page long.

Keep the activity brisk and the discussion lively. Allow everyone to have their say.

Procedure One of the most important aspects of counselling is to ensure that it has been successful. The group is given the following handout and asked to complete it. Once everyone has filled in answers to the questions on the handout, the trainer encourages a discussion of the issues on it and helps the group to clarify its ideas about evaluation of problem-solving and of counselling in general.

Evaluation Each person in turn says what they learnt from the activity and what they will take with them back to 'real life', away from the group.

Closing Participants should be offered a 5-minute period in which to raise questions, express feelings, address particular people in the group or talk through anything else that has arisen from the activity.

EVALUATING PROBLEM-SOLVING

Read through the questions below and make notes next to each. Be prepared to discuss the points that you make when the group reconvenes.

- SHOULD problem-solving be evaluated?
- Why?
- Should COUNSELLING be evaluated?
- HOW can problem-solving be evaluated?
- How can COUNSELLING be evaluated?
- Do you evaluate your own counselling?
- What methods do you use?
- What criteria would you use for evaluating problem-solving?
- How would you use the client's AIMS or GOALS in the evaluation process?
- WHEN would you evaluate problem-solving?
- What would you do if the client's problem-solving strategies had not been successful?

- To what degree is the
  counsellor responsible for
  the outcome of counselling?
- To what degree is the client
  responsible?

BEING SUPPORTIVE

Activity 50

Time required 45 minutes to 1 hour.

Aim To explore personal support in counselling.

Group size Any number between 5 and 25.

Environment A room in which there is space for everyone to sit in a closed circle of chairs and which is large enough for everyone to pair off and spread out, if required. There should be a flipchart and pad or a white/blackboard and marker pens. This is used to jot down comments from group members during discussion periods. Flipchart sheets containing such comments can be pinned to the wall to act as an *aide mémoire*. These can be kept on the wall until the end of the workshop and they help to maintain continuity of content and demonstrate progress.

You may want to present any theoretical points on an acetate sheet, in which case an overhead projector and screen will be required. Any handouts should be prepared prior to using this activity and it is important that there are enough for each person to have one. Reading lists can be given out at the end of the activity and these should be no more than one page long.

Allow everyone to speak and wait until all thoughts and feelings have been shared in the group before moving on to another activity.

Procedure Above almost everything, the counsellor has to be supportive. The befriending and helping role is one of the most important in counselling. This activity helps trainees to explore their own supportiveness and its boundaries.

The group pairs off. One of each pair then reads through the incomplete statements in the enclosed handout and invites their colleagues to complete them. When all the statements have been completed, roles are reversed and the statements are worked through by the other partner.

After everyone has had a turn at completing the statements, the larger group reconvenes. The trainer facilitates a discussion on support in counselling, also inviting the group to consider what support *they* need as counsellors, and discussing the notion of setting up a supervision group or a personal-support network for counsellors in their area.

Evaluation The group is divided into pairs and each pair spends 5 minutes discussing what each person liked and disliked about the activity. The group reforms after 5 minutes and an evaluative discussion is held.

Closing Participants should be offered a 5-minute period in which to raise questions, express feelings, address particular people in the group or talk through anything else that has arisen from the activity.

SUPPORT IN COUNSELLING

Read these incomplete statements to your partner and listen while they complete them. Work through them fairly quickly and do not spend too long on one particular statement. When you have finished, swap roles and repeat the process.

- The most supportive person I know ...
- I could be more supportive if ...
- The problem with being supportive is ...
- I experience being supported when ...
- I used to be supported by ...
- Presently, I am supported by ...
- Too much support can ...
- If I get too dependent on people, I ...
- If I felt I was better supported, I ...
- The limitations of supporting people are ...
- I would not support people if I thought they ...
- The sort of people I could not support are ...
- I feel most supported when ...
- The least supportive people ...
- I need to be supported because ...
- I often support other people because ...

Chapter 12:

Coping with feelings

TYPES OF FEELINGS
Activity 51

Time required 45 minutes to 1 hour.

Aim To explore the range of feelings in a group context.

Group size Any number between 5 and 25.

Environment A room in which there is space for everyone to sit in a closed circle of chairs and which is large enough for everyone to pair off and spread out, if required. There should be a flipchart and pad or a white/blackboard and marker pens. This is used to jot down comments from group members during discussion periods. Flipchart sheets containing such comments can be pinned to the wall to act as an *aide mémoire*. These can be kept on the wall until the end of the workshop and they help to maintain continuity of content and demonstrate progress.

You may want to present any theoretical points on an acetate sheet, in which case an overhead projector and screen will be required. Any handouts should be prepared prior to using this activity and it is important that there are enough for each person to have one. Reading lists can be given out at the end of the activity and these should be no more than one page long.

Encourage everyone to discuss the activity afterwards and make sure that everyone who wants to say something gets the chance.

Procedure The group trainer invites one member to act as 'scribe'. The scribe's task is to write down all the items generated by the group throughout this activity.

The group is invited to call out words that describe 'feelings'. Nothing is to be excluded: all words are permissible. At the end of a prescribed time or when no further words are forthcoming, the trainer helps the group to organize the words into *categories* of feeling. In this way, a considerable range of feelings can be identified and explored in discussion. Examples of categories might be:

- positive feelings;
- negative feelings;
- common feelings;
- unusual feelings;
- difficult feelings.

Evaluation Each person in the group makes notes about what they found useful about the activity. Then an evaluative discussion is held with the trainer as facilitator of that discussion.

Closing Participants should be offered a 5-minute period in which to raise questions, express feelings, address particular people in the group or talk through anything else that has arisen from the activity.

FEELING WORDS
Activity 52

Time required 45 minutes to 1 hour.

Aim To explore individuals' reactions to certain feelings.

Group size Any number between 5 and 25.

Environment A room in which there is space for everyone to sit in a closed circle of chairs and which is large enough for everyone to pair off and spread out, if required. There should be a flipchart and pad or a white/blackboard and marker pens. This is used to jot down comments from group members during discussion periods. Flipchart sheets containing such comments can be pinned to the wall to act as an *aide mémoire*. These can be kept on the wall until the end of the workshop and they help to maintain continuity of content and demonstrate progress.

You may want to present any theoretical points on an acetate sheet, in which case an overhead projector and screen will be required. Any handouts should be prepared prior to using this activity and it is important that there are enough for each person to have one. Reading lists can be given out at the end of the activity and these should be no more than one page long.

Do not hurry people but keep the atmosphere in the group lively and encourage people to share their thoughts and feelings about the activity.

Procedure The group trainer hands out a prepared list of 'feelings'. This could be drawn from the list generated by the previous activity or developed by the trainer. Each person is invited to tick each feeling that they have experienced at some time in their life.

When every person has completed this stage of the activity, group participants are asked to turn to the person on their right and compare notes. After 5 minutes, the larger group reconvenes and a discussion is held about the nature of feelings and the expression of feelings. The group trainer joins in the activity wherever possible.

Evaluation The group is divided into pairs and each pair spends 5 minutes discussing what each person liked and disliked about the activity. The group reforms after 5 minutes and an evaluative discussion is held.

Closing Participants should be offered a 5-minute period in which to raise questions, express feelings, address particular people in the group or talk through anything else that has arisen from the activity.

EXPRESSING FEELINGS
Activity 53

Time required 45 minutes to 1 hour.

Aim To explore group participants' views about the release of emotion.

Group size Any number between 5 and 25.

Environment A room in which there is space for everyone to sit in a closed circle of chairs and which is large enough for everyone to pair off and spread out, if required. There should be a flipchart and pad or a white/blackboard and marker pens. This is used to jot down comments from group members during discussion periods. Flipchart sheets containing such comments can be pinned to the wall to act as an *aide mémoire*. These can be kept on the wall until the end of the workshop and they help to maintain continuity of content and demonstrate progress.

You may want to present any theoretical points on an acetate sheet, in which case an overhead projector and screen will be required. Any handouts should be prepared prior to using this activity and it is important that there are enough for each person to have one. Reading lists can be given out at the end of the activity and these should be no more than one page long.

Allow everyone to speak and wait until all thoughts and feelings have been shared in the group before moving on to another activity.

Procedure The group trainer leads a discussion on the topic 'Coping with Feelings'. Specifically, group members are encouraged to talk about the following issues:

- What sort of feelings is it commonly acceptable to express?
- What are the easiest feelings to cope with when another person expresses them?

● What feelings do *you* have difficulty with?

In this way, the discussion moves from the general and open to the specific and personal. No one should feel compelled to join in the discussion and an 'easy' and light atmosphere is best. If the atmosphere gets too heavy and emotional, the discussion is likely to dry up. Group members' feelings will get in the way of the discussion.

Evaluation Each person in turn says what they learnt from the activity and what they will take with them back to 'real life', away from the group.

Closing Participants should be offered a 5-minute period in which to raise questions, express feelings, address particular people in the group or talk through anything else that has arisen from the activity.

GIVING PERMISSION
Activity 54

Time required 45 minutes to 1 hour.

Aim To explore feelings in a supportive group atmosphere.

Group size Any number between 5 and 25.

Environment A room in which there is space for everyone to sit in a closed circle of chairs and which is large enough for everyone to pair off and spread out, if required. There should be a flipchart and pad or a white/blackboard and marker pens. This is used to jot down comments from group members during discussion periods. Flipchart sheets containing such comments can be pinned to the wall to act as an *aide mémoire*. These can be kept on the wall until the end of the workshop and they help to maintain continuity of content and demonstrate progress.

You may want to present any theoretical points on an acetate sheet, in which case an overhead projector and screen will be required. Any handouts should be prepared prior to using this activity and it is important that there are enough for each person to have one. Reading lists can be given out at the end of the activity and these should be no more than one page long.

Keep the activity brisk and the discussion lively. Allow everyone to have their say.

Procedure This activity is only for use once people know each other fairly well and when the trainer feels able to cope with emotional release.

The activity simply involves the trainer getting group members to express emotion during a discussion or another specific activity. When group members are exploring counselling activities, for example, the trainer may preface the activity by suggesting that it become a group norm that people be allowed to laugh, cry or get angry during the activity. If this *does* happen, it is important that full support is given to the person who expresses emotion. Such support is given by allowing full release of the emotion followed by a quiet period in which the person is allowed and encouraged to 'make sense' of what has happened. This period is sometimes known as 'debriefing' and is an essential part of any activity that involves the free expression of feelings.

The group trainer always joins in the activity and may serve as a role model in being prepared to express appropriate emotion during an activity.

Evaluation Two 'rounds' are conducted. In the first round, each person in turn says what they liked *least* about the activity. In the second, each person in turn says what they liked *most* about the activity. The trainer joins in this evaluation process and decides whether or not there is a discussion of the points that are raised.

Closing Participants should be offered a 5-minute period in which to raise questions, express feelings, address particular people in the group or talk through anything else that has arisen from the activity.

PARADOX

Activity 55

Time required 45 minutes to 1 hour.

Aim To explore the paradoxical nature of feelings.

Group size Any number between 5 and 25.

Environment A room in which there is space for everyone to sit in a closed circle of chairs and which is large enough for everyone to pair off and spread out, if required. There should be a flipchart and pad or a white/blackboard and marker pens. This is used to jot down comments from group members during discussion periods. Flipchart sheets containing such comments can be pinned to the wall to act as an *aide mémoire*. These can be kept on the wall until the end of the workshop and they help to maintain continuity of content and demonstrate progress.

You may want to present any theoretical points on an acetate sheet, in which case an overhead projector and screen will be required. Any handouts should be prepared prior to using this activity and it is important that there are enough for each person to have one. Reading lists can be given out at the end of the activity and these should be no more than one page long.

Allow everyone to speak and wait until all thoughts and feelings have been shared in the group before moving on to another activity.

Procedure We often seem to say exactly the opposite of what we really feel. For this activity, the trainer merely makes use of a strategy for exploring this paradox. During a discussion in which feelings are being discussed, the trainer occasionally asks a group member to explore the 'opposite pole' of the expressed feeling by reversing the statement they have made. Thus, the trainer will use the expression 'try saying the opposite of that' after a group member has expressed a particular feeling. Here is an example of the trainer's intervention in action.

I'm quite relaxed about this. Nothing bothers me about it at all . . .

Try saying the opposite of that.

I'm not at all relaxed . . . How odd! I'm not really relaxed at all!

Evaluation Each person in the group makes notes about what they found useful about the activity. Then an evaluative discussion is held with the trainer as facilitator of that discussion.

Closing Participants should be offered a 5-minute period in which to raise questions, express feelings, address particular people in the group or talk through anything else that has arisen from the activity.

FOCUSING

Activity 56

Time required 45 minutes to 1 hour.

Aim To explore a particular type of problem-solving through focusing.

Group size Any number between 5 and 25.

Environment A room in which there is space for everyone to sit in a closed circle of chairs and which is large enough for everyone to pair off and spread out, if required. There should be a flipchart and pad or a white/blackboard and marker pens. This is used to jot down comments from group members during discussion periods. Flipchart sheets containing such comments can be pinned to the wall to act as an *aide mémoire*. These can be kept on the wall until the end of the workshop and they help to maintain continuity of content and demonstrate progress.

You may want to present any theoretical points on an acetate sheet, in which case an overhead projector and screen will be required. Any handouts should be prepared prior to using this activity and it is important that there are enough for each person to have one. Reading lists can be given out at the end of the activity and these should be no more than one page long.

Encourage everyone to discuss the activity afterwards and make sure that everyone who wants to say something gets the chance.

Procedure Focusing is a simple method of problem-solving through relaxation and through focusing on feelings. This is a simple process of allowing the body and mind to relax and thus enabling a 'felt sense' of one's problems to emerge. The process allows for a natural process of problem-solving to occur. The focusing approach outlined here is based on that described by

Eugene Gendlin (1981). The group trainer uses these instructions to lead the group through the process of focusing.

Evaluation Each person in turn says what they learnt from the activity and what they will take with them back to 'real life', away from the group.

Closing Participants should be offered a 5-minute period in which to raise questions, express feelings, address particular people in the group or talk through anything else that has arisen from the activity.

FOCUSING

1. Sit quietly and breathe deeply for a while. Allow yourself to relax completely. Notice the thoughts and feelings that flood into your mind. Slowly, but without worrying too much, identify each one.

2. Having identified each thought or feeling that comes drifting into your mind, find some way of 'packaging up' each of those thoughts and feelings. Some people find it easiest to imagine actually wrapping up each issue into a parcel. Others imagine putting each item into a box and sealing it with tape. However you do it, allow each thought or feeling to be packaged in some way. Then imagine those thoughts or feelings, in their packages, laid out in front of you. Notice, too, the sense of calmness that goes with having packaged up your thoughts and feelings in this way.

3. Now, in your mind, look around at those packages and notice which one of them is calling for attention. Sometimes there will be more than one but try to focus on the one that is *most* in need.

4. Now unpack that one particular issue and allow it some breathing space. Do not immediately put a name to it or rush to 'sort it out'. Instead, allow yourself to become immersed in that particular issue.

5. When you have spent some minutes immersing yourself in this way, ask yourself : 'what is the *feeling* that goes with this issue?' Don't rush to put a label to it: try one or two labels, tentatively at first. Allow the label to 'emerge' out of the issue. This feeling that emerges in this way can be described as the 'felt sense' of the issue or problem.

6. Once you have identified this 'felt sense' in this way, allow yourself to explore it for a while. What other feelings go with it? What other thoughts do you associate with it? And so on.

7. Once you have explored the felt sense in this way, ask yourself: what is the *nub of all this*? As you ask this, allow the real issue

behind all your thoughts to emerge and to surface. Often, the nub or 'bottom line' is a quite different issue to the one that you started out with.

8. When you have identified the nub or the crux of the issue, allow yourself to explore that a little. Then identify what it is you have to do next. Do not do this too hastily. Again, try out a number of solutions before you settle on what has to be done. Do not rush to make up your mind but rather let the next step emerge of its own accord. Once you have identified the next thing that you have to do, acknowledge to yourself that this is the end of the activity for the time being.

9. Allow yourself some more deep breaths. Relax quietly and then rouse yourself gently.

After: Gendlin, E. (1981) *Focusing*, Bantam, New York.

EXAGGERATION
Activity 57

Time required 45 minutes to 1 hour.

Aim To explore feelings in a group setting.

Group size Any number between 5 and 25.

Environment A room in which there is space for everyone to sit in a closed circle of chairs and which is large enough for everyone to pair off and spread out, if required. There should be a flipchart and pad or a white/blackboard and marker pens. This is used to jot down comments from group members during discussion periods. Flipchart sheets containing such comments can be pinned to the wall to act as an *aide mémoire*. These can be kept on the wall until the end of the workshop and they help to maintain continuity of content and demonstrate progress.

You may want to present any theoretical points on an acetate sheet, in which case an overhead projector and screen will be required. Any handouts should be prepared prior to using this activity and it is important that there are enough for each person to have one. Reading lists can be given out at the end of the activity and these should be no more than one page long.

Do not hurry people but keep the atmosphere in the group lively and encourage people to share their thoughts and feelings about the activity.

Procedure This sounds an odd activity when it is put down in black and white! All that is involved is that during a particular discussion of any topic related to feelings, group participants are asked to exaggerate the way they feel about what is under discussion. Thus, the person who feels slightly irritated, acts as if very irritated; the person who is cheered by something that is said, laughs wholeheartedly about the issue. This form of exaggeration is sometimes described as 'acting in' to feelings. Sometimes, too, the exaggeration leads to the expression of real feeling. If it does not, it allows group participants to consider a range of ways of thinking about feelings and about helping other people who express them. This activity is a particular sort of role play and requires the debriefing period described in Activity 54. The group trainer always joins in the activity.

Evaluation The group is divided into pairs and each pair spends 5 minutes discussing what each person liked and disliked about the activity. The group reforms after 5 minutes and an evaluative discussion is held.

Closing Participants should be offered a 5-minute period in which to raise questions, express feelings, address particular people in the group or talk through anything else that has arisen from the activity.

EARLIEST MEMORY
Activity 58

Time required 45 minutes to 1 hour.

Aim To explore the possible genesis of some of our feelings.

Group size Any number between 5 and 25.

Environment A room in which there is space for everyone to sit in a closed circle of chairs and which is large enough for everyone to pair off and spread out, if required. There should be a flipchart and pad or a white/blackboard and marker pens. This is used to jot down comments from group members during discussion periods. Flipchart sheets containing such comments can be pinned to the wall to act as an *aide mémoire*. These can be kept on the wall until the end of the workshop and they help to maintain continuity of content and demonstrate progress.

You may want to present any theoretical points on an acetate sheet, in which case an overhead projector and screen will be required. Any handouts should be prepared prior to using this activity and it is important that there are enough for each person to have one. Reading lists can be given out at the end of the activity and these should be no more than one page long.

Keep the activity brisk and the discussion lively. Allow everyone to have their say.

Procedure The psychodynamic school of psychology argues that our feelings in adulthood are linked to early childhood experiences.

For this activity, the trainer invites group members to recall their earliest remembrances and encourages each group member to relate that experience to the group. The trainer allows each person to describe the feelings that are associated with the early memory and then encourages that person to think about how those early memories and their associated feelings link with the present.

This can either be carried out as a 'round' in which each person recalls an early experience in turn, or it can be run more informally with group members participating as they remember things. The group trainer joins in the activity wherever possible.

Evaluation Two 'rounds' are conducted. In the first round, each person in turn says what they liked *least* about the activity. In the second, each person in turn says what they liked *most* about the activity. The trainer joins in this evaluation process and decides whether or not there is a discussion of the points that are raised.

Closing Participants should be offered a 5-minute period in which to raise questions, express feelings, address particular people in the group or talk through anything else that has arisen from the activity.

PREVENTING BURNOUT

Activity 59

Time required 45 minutes to 1 hour.

Aim To explore ways of preventing burnout in counselling.

Group size Any number between 5 and 25.

Environment A room in which there is space for everyone to sit in a closed circle of chairs and which is large enough for everyone to pair off and spread out, if required. There should be a flipchart and pad or a white/blackboard and marker pens. This is used to jot down comments from group members during discussion periods. Flipchart sheets containing such comments can be pinned to the wall to act as an *aide mémoire*. These can be kept on the wall until the end of the workshop and they help to maintain continuity of content and demonstrate progress.

You may want to present any theoretical points on an acetate sheet, in which case an overhead projector and screen will be required. Any handouts should be prepared prior to using this activity and it is important that there are enough for each person to have one. Reading lists can be given out at the end of the activity and these should be no more than one page long.

Do not hurry people but keep the atmosphere in the group lively and encourage people to share their thoughts and feelings about the activity.

Procedure Counselling is hard work. Listening to other people's problems can lead to burnout. This has been described as emotional and physical exhaustion as a result of work-related and people-related occupations. The counsellor is particularly prone to burnout.

The aim of this activity is to allow group participants to explore ways of preventing such burnout. The group divides into smaller sub-groups of four or five. The sub-groups then brainstorm methods of preventing burnout. Their methods are written by a scribe on to flipchart sheets. Examples of items brainstormed by groups who have carried out this activity include:

- Talking things through with a colleague.
- Taking a break.
- Only doing a small amount of counselling.
- Only dealing with one client at a time.
- Using relaxation methods.
- Meditation.
- Doing a very different sort of work when not counselling.
- Listening to music.
- Life planning and management.
- Managing time.
- Expressing feelings to another person.
- Sport.

After 15 minutes, the larger group reconvenes and the flipchart sheets are displayed on the floor in the middle of the group. The trainer encourages group members to share their ideas and to formulate plans for preventing burnout in their own counselling practice.

Evaluation Each person in the group makes notes about what they found useful about the activity. Then an evaluative discussion is held with the trainer as facilitator of that discussion.

Closing Participants should be offered a 5-minute period in which to raise questions, express feelings, address particular people in the group or talk through anything else that has arisen from the activity.

COPING WITH STRESS

Activity 60

Time required 45 minutes to 1 hour.

Aim To explore one means of reducing stress.

Group size Any number between 5 and 25.

Environment A room in which there is space for everyone to sit in a closed circle of chairs and which is large enough for everyone to pair off and spread out, if required. There should be a flipchart and pad or a white/blackboard and marker pens. This is used to jot down comments from group members during discussion periods. Flipchart sheets containing such comments can be pinned to the wall to act as an *aide mémoire*. These can be kept on the wall until the end of the workshop and they help to maintain continuity of content and demonstrate progress.

You may want to present any theoretical points on an acetate sheet, in which case an overhead projector and screen will be required. Any handouts should be prepared prior to using this activity and it is important that there are enough for each person to have one. Reading lists can be given out at the end of the activity and these should be no more than one page long.

Allow everyone to speak and wait until all thoughts and feelings have been shared in the group before moving on to another activity.

Procedure This is a straightforward stress-reduction script which can be read out at any workshop in which people want to learn one way of reducing stress. It can also be used to close a difficult or emotional workshop. The trainer reads out the following script while the trainees lie spread out on the floor.

This script encourages you to imagine what it feels like *inside* your body and to relax almost from the 'inside out'!

Lie on your back with your hands by your sides ... stretch your legs out and have your feet about a foot apart ... pay attention to your breathing ... take two or three deep breaths ... breathe in through the nose ... and out through the mouth ... now let your breathing become gentle and relaxed ... now I want you to become aware of your body ... starting at the toes ... try to experience the feeling in your feet and toes ... try to experience that as though you were inside *your feet and toes ... now become aware of the lower parts of your legs ... as if from the inside ... now your knees ... become aware of your joints ... become aware of your thighs and the tops of your legs ... experience them as if you were inside them ... now experience your pelvis and hips ... now your abdomen ... as if from the inside ... put your attention into your chest ... experience the feeling inside your chest ... now your hands ... your lower arms ... your upper arms ... imagine being inside your arms ... now experience your shoulders ... feel the shoulder joints ... experience the feeling inside your neck ... the back of your head ... now your head itself ... feel and experience your face ... the muscles in your face ... your lips ... your nose ... your eyes ... finally ... your scalp ... imagine the feeling as though you were beneath your scalp ... remain fully aware of all parts of your body ... notice which parts you can fully experience ... and which parts are numb to you ... see if you can become more aware of those parts of your body ... now just lie and relax for a few more moments ... take a couple of deep breaths ... and slowly ... in your own time ... sit up and open your eyes.*

Evaluation The group is divided into pairs and each pair spends 5 minutes discussing what each person liked and disliked about the activity. The group reforms after 5 minutes and an evaluative discussion is held.

Closing Participants should be offered a 5-minute period in which to raise questions, express feelings, address particular people in the group or talk through anything else that has arisen from the activity.

Chapter 13:

Evaluation activities

SELF-MONITORING
Activity 61

Time required 45 minutes to 1 hour.

Aim To help trainees monitor their own progress as counsellors.

Group size Any number between 5 and 25.

Environment A room in which there is space for everyone to sit in a closed circle of chairs and which is large enough for everyone to pair off and spread out, if required. There should be a flipchart and pad or a white/blackboard and marker pens. This is used to jot down comments from group members during discussion periods. Flipchart sheets containing such comments can be pinned to the wall to act as an *aide mémoire*. These can be kept on the wall until the end of the workshop and they help to maintain continuity of content and demonstrate progress.

You may want to present any theoretical points on an acetate sheet, in which case an overhead projector and screen will be required. Any handouts should be prepared prior to using this activity and it is important that there are enough for each person to have one. Reading lists can be given out at the end of the activity and these should be no more than one page long.

Encourage everyone to discuss the activity afterwards and make sure that everyone who wants to say something gets the chance.

Procedure The group divides into pairs and together they work through the handout that accompanies this activity by making notes under the various questions. After all participants have completed their questions, they return to the larger group. The trainer then encourages a discussion of how participants might monitor their progress as counsellors.

Evaluation Two 'rounds' are conducted. In the first round, each person in turn says what they liked *least* about the activity. In the second, each person in turn says what they liked *most* about the activity. The trainer joins in this evaluation process and decides whether or not there is a discussion of the points that are raised.

Closing Participants should be offered a 5-minute period in which to raise questions, express feelings, address particular people in the group or talk through anything else that has arisen from the activity.

MONITORING PROGRESS

It is important to reflect continually on your progress in counselling. Read through the following questions and, after discussion with your partner, make notes under each of them.

- What else do you need to do to enhance your listening skills?
- To what degree are you currently functioning as an effective counsellor?
- What other counselling skills do you need to practise?
- What sort of counsellor would you like to be?
- What are the basic skills of counselling?
- Do you have them?
- What are the most difficult parts of counselling for you?
- What do you most like about other people's counselling?
- What situations would you most like to avoid in counselling?
- What will you do to monitor your own progress?
- What other training will you seek out?
- Could you imagine forming a counsellor-support group?
- Will you meet other people in this group once this workshop has finished?
- If so, what definite plans have you made in this direction?

SELF-EVALUATION
Activity 62

Time required 45 minutes to 1 hour.

Aim To enable trainees to self-evaluate their counselling skills.

Group size Any number between 5 and 25.

Environment A room in which there is space for everyone to sit in a closed circle of chairs and which is large enough for everyone to pair off and spread out, if required. There should be a flipchart and pad or a white/blackboard and marker pens. This is used to jot down comments from group members during discussion periods. Flipchart sheets containing such comments can be pinned to the wall to act as an *aide mémoire*. These can be kept on the wall until the end of the workshop and they help to maintain continuity of content and demonstrate progress.

You may want to present any theoretical points on an acetate sheet, in which case an overhead projector and screen will be required. Any handouts should be prepared prior to using this activity and it is important that there are enough for each person to have one. Reading lists can be given out at the end of the activity and these should be no more than one page long.

Keep the activity brisk and the discussion lively. Allow everyone to have their say.

Procedure Each trainee is given the questionnaire that accompanies this activity and is asked to complete it. Afterwards, the group convenes and there is a discussion of each of the items on the questionnaire.

Evaluation Each person in turn says what they learnt from the activity and what they will take with them back to 'real life', away from the group.

Closing Participants should be offered a 5-minute period in which to raise questions, express feelings, address particular people in the group or talk through anything else that has arisen from the activity.

COUNSELLING SELF-EVALUATION QUESTIONNAIRE

Read through the following statements and tick the most appropriate answers to each. Respond to all the statements and try not to tick the 'don't know' boxes unless you really cannot decide. Be prepared to discuss your answers in the group.

1. I need a lot more practice as a counsellor.

Strongly Agree	Agree	Don't Know	Disagree	Strongly Disagree	Leave Blank

2. I work well as a counsellor.

Strongly Agree	Agree	Don't Know	Disagree	Strongly Disagree	Leave Blank

3. I intend to develop my training and education as a counsellor.

Strongly Agree	Agree	Don't Know	Disagree	Strongly Disagree	Leave Blank

4. Other people in the group function more effectively as counsellors than I seem to.

Strongly Agree	Agree	Don't Know	Disagree	Strongly Disagree	Leave Blank

5. It is important to monitor continually your own progress as a counsellor.

Strongly Agree	Agree	Don't Know	Disagree	Strongly Disagree	Leave Blank

6. I often reflect on my skills and deficits as a counsellor.

Strongly Agree	Agree	Don't Know	Disagree	Strongly Disagree	Leave Blank

7. You can become very introspective when you work as a counsellor.

Strongly Agree	Agree	Don't Know	Disagree	Strongly Disagree	Leave Blank

8. I enjoy working as a counsellor.

Strongly Agree	Agree	Don't Know	Disagree	Strongly Disagree	Leave Blank

9. I can see myself working as a counsellor in five years' time.

Strongly Agree	Agree	Don't Know	Disagree	Strongly Disagree	Leave Blank

10. Counselling skills are just a set of useful communication skills that can be used in any work-related situation.

Strongly Agree	Agree	Don't Know	Disagree	Strongly Disagree	Leave Blank

11. I would not like to deal with too much emotional distress in counselling.

Strongly Agree	Agree	Don't Know	Disagree	Strongly Disagree	Leave Blank

12. Other people seem to think I counsel well.

Strongly Agree	Agree	Don't Know	Disagree	Strongly Disagree	Leave Blank

13. I often compare myself to other people.

Strongly Agree	Agree	Don't Know	Disagree	Strongly Disagree	Leave Blank

14. I am reasonably confident in the role of counsellor.

Strongly Agree	Agree	Don't Know	Disagree	Strongly Disagree	Leave Blank

15. Counselling is a 'fashionable' activity and the interest in it will soon wane.

Strongly Agree	Agree	Don't Know	Disagree	Strongly Disagree	Leave Blank

16. I am improving my counselling skills all the time.

Strongly Agree	Agree	Don't Know	Disagree	Strongly Disagree	Leave Blank

17. I have improved as a counsellor during the life of this workshop.

Strongly Agree	Agree	Don't Know	Disagree	Strongly Disagree	Leave Blank

PEER EVALUATION
Activity 63

Time required 45 minutes to 1 hour.

Aim To encourage group participants to give each other feedback.

Group size Any number between 5 and 25.

Environment A room in which there is space for everyone to sit in a closed circle of chairs and which is large enough for everyone to pair off and spread out, if required. There should be a flipchart and pad or a white/blackboard and marker pens. This is used to jot down comments from group members during discussion periods. Flipchart sheets containing such comments can be pinned to the wall to act as an *aide mémoire*. These can be kept on the wall until the end of the workshop and they help to maintain continuity of content and demonstrate progress.

You may want to present any theoretical points on an acetate sheet, in which case an overhead projector and screen will be required. Any handouts should be prepared prior to using this activity and it is important that there are enough for each person to have one. Reading lists can be given out at the end of the activity and these should be no more than one page long.

Keep the activity brisk and the discussion lively. Allow everyone to have their say.

Procedure Each trainee is given the questionnaire that accompanies this activity and is asked to complete it. Afterwards, the group convenes and there is a discussion of each of the items on the questionnaire.

Evaluation The group is divided into pairs and each pair spends 5 minutes discussing what each person liked and disliked about the activity. The group reforms after 5 minutes and an evaluative discussion is held.

Closing Participants should be offered a 5-minute period in which to raise questions, express feelings, address particular people in the group or talk through anything else that has arisen from the activity.

PEER EVALUATION QUESTIONNAIRE

Consider the members of this group and then complete the following questionnaire. Fill in the names of AT LEAST TWO PEOPLE for each question.

QUESTION	GROUP MEMBERS
1. Which members of the group are the best listeners?	
2. Which members of the group tend to talk most?	
3. Who are the quietest members of the group?	

QUESTION	GROUP MEMBERS
4. Which group members are MOST SIMILAR to you?	
5. Which group members are MOST DIFFERENT to you?	
6. Which three group members do you consider to be the most skilled counsellors, so far?	

QUESTION	GROUP MEMBERS
7. Which group members do you think are most likely to be effective counsellors after this workshop?	
8. Who are the people that you have learned most from?	
9. Which two group members would you choose to be counselled by?	

QUESTION	GROUP MEMBERS
10. Which group members would you most like to spend the evening with?	

PAIRS EVALUATION
Activity 64

Time required 45 minutes to 1 hour.

Aim To evaluate a group workshop in a pairs format.

Group size Any number between 5 and 25.

Environment A room in which there is space for everyone to sit in a closed circle of chairs and which is large enough for everyone to pair off and spread out, if required. There should be a flipchart and pad or a white/blackboard and marker pens. This is used to jot down comments from group members during discussion periods. Flipchart sheets containing such comments can be pinned to the wall to act as an *aide mémoire*. These can be kept on the wall until the end of the workshop and they help to maintain continuity of content and demonstrate progress.

You may want to present any theoretical points on an acetate sheet, in which case an overhead projector and screen will be required. Any handouts should be prepared prior to using this activity and it is important that there are enough for each person to have one. Reading lists can be given out at the end of the activity and these should be no more than one page long.

Do not hurry people but keep the atmosphere in the group lively and encourage people to share their thoughts and feelings about the activity.

Procedure The group pairs off. Each pair nominates one as 'A' and one as 'B'. 'A' then evaluates the workshop to 'B' in terms of the following criteria:

- Content.
- Teaching/learning experiences.

- Things learned.
- My contribution.

When 'A' has evaluated in this way, the pairs swap roles and 'B' evaluates the workshop, using the above criteria, to 'A'.

The trainer invites the larger group to reconvene. Then, a discussion is held about the activity. Two facets are discussed: the *process* of the activity (what it felt like to do it) and the *content* (what was talked about during the activity). As always, the process is more important than the content and, sometimes, the trainer may choose to discuss *only* the process. Also, the trainer helps the group to identify ways in which what has been learnt from the activity can be related to the group members' professional or personal life. The group trainer joins in the activity wherever possible.

Evaluation Each person in the group makes notes about what they found useful about the activity. Then an evaluative discussion is held with the trainer as facilitator of that discussion.

Closing Participants should be offered a 5-minute period in which to raise questions, express feelings, address particular people in the group or talk through anything else that has arisen from the activity.

NOMINAL GROUP EVALUATION

Activity 65

Time required 45 minutes to 1 hour.

Aim To evaluate a group, workshop or course.

Group size Any number between 5 and 25.

Environment A room in which there is space for everyone to sit in a closed circle of chairs and which is large enough for everyone to pair off and spread out, if required. There should be a flipchart and pad or a white/blackboard and marker pens. This is used to jot down comments from group members during discussion periods. Flipchart sheets containing such comments can be pinned to the wall to act as an *aide mémoire*. These can be kept on the wall until the end of the workshop and they help to maintain continuity of content and demonstrate progress.

You may want to present any theoretical points on an acetate sheet, in which case an overhead projector and screen will be required. Any handouts should be prepared prior to using this activity and it is important that there are enough for each person to have one. Reading lists can be given out at the end of the activity and these should be no more than one page long.

Encourage everyone to discuss the activity afterwards and make sure that everyone who wants to say something gets the chance.

Procedure The group trainer invites the group to 'brainstorm' aspects of the course that they have found useful, using the brainstorming technique described elsewhere in this book. Examples of such items might be:

• the theory input on group dynamics;

- the discussion on Tuesday, about self awareness;
- the chance to work in pairs, etc.

These items, as they are identified, are written on to a blackboard or flipchart pad.

When the brainstorming has been completed, each person is invited to go to the board or pad and tick three items with which they most strongly agree. The 'most ticked' items are then discussed within the group.

Evaluation Two 'rounds' are conducted. In the first round, each person in turn says what they liked *least* about the activity. In the second, each person in turn says what they liked *most* about the activity. The trainer joins in this evaluation process and decides whether or not there is a discussion of the points that are raised.

Closing Participants should be offered a 5-minute period in which to raise questions, express feelings, address particular people in the group or talk through anything else that has arisen from the activity.

SELF AND PEER EVALUATION
Activity 66

Time required 45 minutes to 1 hour.

Aim To evaluate a workshop or course.

Group size Any number between 5 and 25.

Environment A room in which there is space for everyone to sit in a closed circle of chairs and which is large enough for everyone to pair off and spread out, if required. There should be a flipchart and pad or a white/blackboard and marker pens. This is used to jot down comments from group members during discussion periods. Flipchart sheets containing such comments can be pinned to the wall to act as an *aide mémoire*. These can be kept on the wall until the end of the workshop and they help to maintain continuity of content and demonstrate progress.

You may want to present any theoretical points on an acetate sheet, in which case an overhead projector and screen will be required. Any handouts should be prepared prior to using this activity and it is important that there are enough for each person to have one. Reading lists can be given out at the end of the activity and these should be no more than one page long.

Keep the activity brisk and the discussion lively. Allow everyone to have their say.

Procedure The first part of this activity is the self-evaluation element, the second is the peer-evaluation element.

One group member starts the activity by reviewing, to the group, his or her contribution to the group, workshop or course, as thoroughly as possible. This is done initially without comment from colleagues or trainer.

Next, that person invites one of the following sorts of feedback about their role in the group, workshop or course:

- positive aspects;
- negative aspects;
- both positive and negative.

Examples of such feedback comments might be:

- *I appreciated your ability to break up arguments when they occurred in the group.*
- *I liked the way you supported people.*
- *I would have preferred you to join in some of the activities a little more.*

Once one member of the group has undertaken both self and peer evaluation in this way, the next person goes through the same cycle until everyone in the room has completed both elements of the activity. The group trainer joins in the activity wherever possible and undertakes both aspects of self and peer evaluation.

Evaluation Each person in turn says what they learnt from the activity and what they will take with them back to 'real life', away from the group.

Closing Participants should be offered a 5-minute period in which to raise questions, express feelings, address particular people in the group or talk through anything else that has arisen from the activity.

JOURNAL

Activity 67

Time required 45 minutes to 1 hour.

Aim To evaluate a workshop or course.

Group size Any number between 5 and 25.

Environment A room in which there is space for everyone to sit in a closed circle of chairs and which is large enough for everyone to pair off and spread out, if required. There should be a flipchart and pad or a white/blackboard and marker pens. This is used to jot down comments from group members during discussion periods. Flipchart sheets containing such comments can be pinned to the wall to act as an *aide mémoire*. These can be kept on the wall until the end of the workshop and they help to maintain continuity of content and demonstrate progress.

You may want to present any theoretical points on an acetate sheet, in which case an overhead projector and screen will be required. Any handouts should be prepared prior to using this activity and it is important that there are enough for each person to have one. Reading lists can be given out at the end of the activity and these should be no more than one page long.

Allow everyone to speak and wait until all thoughts and feelings have been shared in the group before moving on to another activity.

Procedure At the beginning of the group, course or workshop, each person is encouraged to keep a journal. The journal can be a notebook or ring binder with loose sheets. The following headings are used as the means of keeping notes after each meeting of the group or each day of the course or workshop:

- Things learned today.
- Teaching and learning methods.

- Reflections on my own contribution.
- New references to journal articles or books.
- Other notes.

The journal can then be used as an evaluation device in one or more of the following ways:

- As a discussion document for use in a group meeting at the beginning of each day of a workshop or course.
- As a focus of discussion in the final hour or two of a workshop or course.
- As material for a written evaluation handed in by each participant at the end of a series of group meetings, a workshop or a course.

The group trainer joins in the activity wherever possible and also keeps a journal.

Evaluation The group is divided into pairs and each pair spends 5 minutes discussing what each person liked and disliked about the activity. The group reforms after 5 minutes and an evaluative discussion is held.

Closing Participants should be offered a 5-minute period in which to raise questions, express feelings, address particular people in the group or talk through anything else that has arisen from the activity.

LEAST AND MOST
Activity 68

Time required 45 minutes to 1 hour.

Aim To undertake an 'instant' evaluation of an activity, course or workshop.

Group size Any number between 5 and 25.

Environment A large room in which people can sit comfortably in a group. Chairs should be of equal height and the group should remain in a closed circle throughout the activity. The trainer should be part of that circle. No special equipment is required for this activity.

Procedure This activity can be used after a particular group activity, a course or a workshop.

Each person, in turn, finishes two sentences, as follows:

● What I liked *least* about the [activity, day, workshop] was ...
● What I liked *most* about the [activity, day, workshop] was ...

The group trainer joins in the activity wherever possible and says what he or she liked least and most about the activity, day or workshop.

Evaluation Each person in the group makes notes about what they found useful about the activity. Then an evaluative discussion is held with the trainer as facilitator of that discussion.

Closing Participants should be offered a 5-minute period in which to raise questions, express feelings, address particular people in the group or talk through anything else that has arisen from the activity.

THINGS LEARNT
Activity 69

Time required 45 minutes to 1 hour.

Aim To evaluate an activity, workshop or course.

Group size Any number between 5 and 25.

Environment A room in which there is space for everyone to sit in a closed circle of chairs and which is large enough for everyone to pair off and spread out, if required. There should be a flipchart and pad or a white/blackboard and marker pens. This is used to jot down comments from group members during discussion periods. Flipchart sheets containing such comments can be pinned to the wall to act as an *aide mémoire*. These can be kept on the wall until the end of the workshop and they help to maintain continuity of content and demonstrate progress.

You may want to present any theoretical points on an acetate sheet, in which case an overhead projector and screen will be required. Any handouts should be prepared prior to using this activity and it is important that there are enough for each person to have one. Reading lists can be given out at the end of the activity and these should be no more than one page long.

Procedure Each person in turn states three things they learnt from an activity within the group or from the workshop or course. The group trainer joins in the activity wherever possible and also offers examples of three things that he or she learnt.

Evaluation Each person in turn says what they learnt from the activity and what they will take with them back to 'real life', away from the group.

Closing Participants should be offered a 5-minute period in which to raise questions, express feelings, address particular people in the group or talk through anything else that has arisen from the activity.

FUTURE PLANNING
Activity 70

Time required 45 minutes to 1 hour.

Aim To enable course or workshop trainees to plan their futures.

Group size Any number between 5 and 25.

Environment A room in which there is space for everyone to sit in a closed circle of chairs and which is large enough for everyone to pair off and spread out, if required. There should be a flipchart and pad or a white/blackboard and marker pens. This is used to jot down comments from group members during discussion periods. Flipchart sheets containing such comments can be pinned to the wall to act as an *aide mémoire*. These can be kept on the wall until the end of the workshop and they help to maintain continuity of content and demonstrate progress.

You may want to present any theoretical points on an acetate sheet, in which case an overhead projector and screen will be required. Any handouts should be prepared prior to using this activity and it is important that there are enough for each person to have one. Reading lists can be given out at the end of the activity and these should be no more than one page long.

Do not hurry people but keep the atmosphere in the group lively and encourage people to share their thoughts and feelings about the activity.

Procedure An amount of time is set aside each day (or at the end of a group meeting) for this activity.

The 'Quaker group' approach is used (see Activity 74). First, members of the group are invited to state what activities they want to take part in during the next meeting of the group, workshop or course. After each item is raised by a group member, other members are allowed to 'modify' the suggestion in any way in order to suit their own interests. If no other 'modifications' are offered, the group moves on to another suggestion. Here is an example of a proposal and its modifications, using this approach:

- *I suggest that we have a lengthy discussion, tomorrow, on the question of how we deal with anger in the group . . .*
- *I suggest we limit the discussion to a half-hour period . . .*
- *I would like to sit out on that discussion altogether . . .*
- *I think we should all take part in it . . .*
- Silence
- Trainer: *The proposal is carried that we should all take part in a discussion about how we deal with anger.*

Evaluation Two 'rounds' are conducted. In the first round, each person in turn says what they liked *least* about the activity. In the second, each person in turn says what they liked *most* about the activity. The trainer joins in this evaluation process and decides whether or not there is a discussion of the points that are raised.

Closing Participants should be offered a 5-minute period in which to raise questions, express feelings, address particular people in the group or talk through anything else that has arisen from the activity.

Chapter 14:

Counsellor-development activities

COUNSELLING-SKILLS ASSESSMENT

Activity 71

Time required 45 minutes to 1 hour.

Aim To enable counselling-workshop participants to assess their own counselling skills and their views about counselling.

Group size Any number between 5 and 25.

Environment A room in which there is space for everyone to sit in a closed circle of chairs and which is large enough for everyone to pair off and spread out, if required. There should be a flipchart and pad or a white/blackboard and marker pens. This is used to jot down comments from group members during discussion periods. Flipchart sheets containing such comments can be pinned to the wall to act as an *aide mémoire*. These can be kept on the wall until the end of the workshop and they help to maintain continuity of content and demonstrate progress.

You may want to present any theoretical points on an acetate sheet, in which case an overhead projector and screen will be required. Any handouts should be prepared prior to using this activity and it is important that there are enough for each person to have one. Reading lists can be given out at the end of the activity and these should be no more than one page long.

Encourage everyone to discuss the activity afterwards and make sure that everyone who wants to say something gets the chance.

Procedure Each participant is given a copy of the questionnaire that follows these instructions. They are asked to complete the questionnaire by working through it fairly quickly. After the questionnaires have been filled in, the trainer has two choices. First, the instrument can be used as a focus of discussion. There are no right or wrong answers to each of the items but varied responses can encourage lively debate. Alternatively, participants can 'score' their questionnaires by putting a figure in each of the 'leave blank' spaces on the questionnaire boxes. Each item is scored as follows:

Strongly Agree	Agree	Don't Know	Disagree	Strongly Disagree	Leave Blank
Scores 5	Scores 4	Scores 3	Scores 2	Scores 1	

Once all items have been scored in this way, the trainer uses the *scoresheet* to collate the various scores. On the scoresheet, the trainer identifies the number of participants who said they strongly agreed, agreed, didn't know, disagreed and strongly disagreed to each item. The scoresheet thus offers a consensus view of how participants felt about each item. This completed scoresheet can then be photocopied and handed out to participants for discussion.

Evaluation Each person in turn says first what they liked *least* about the activity, then each person in turn says what they liked *most* about the activity. The group leader or facilitator joins in this activity.

Closing Participants should be offered a 5-minute period in which to raise questions, express feelings, address particular people in the group or talk through anything else that has arisen from the activity.

COUNSELLING-SKILLS ASSESSMENT QUESTIONNAIRE

Read through each of the statements and then tick a box. You may strongly agree, agree, disagree or strongly disagree with each statement. You may also indicate that you 'don't know' about a particular item. Work fairly quickly through the statements; do not miss any out.

1. On the whole, I am a fairly effective counsellor.

Strongly Agree	Agree	Don't Know	Disagree	Strongly Disagree	Leave Blank

2. I have had a considerable amount of practice as a counsellor.

Strongly Agree	Agree	Don't Know	Disagree	Strongly Disagree	Leave Blank

3. Given the chance, I would undertake another course in counselling.

Strongly Agree	Agree	Don't Know	Disagree	Strongly Disagree	Leave Blank

4. I am an effective listener.

Strongly Agree	Agree	Don't Know	Disagree	Strongly Disagree	Leave Blank

© P. Burnard 1992, published by Kogan Page

5. As a counsellor, I tend to talk too much.

Strongly Agree	Agree	Don't Know	Disagree	Strongly Disagree	Leave Blank

6. I use counselling skills every day.

Strongly Agree	Agree	Don't Know	Disagree	Strongly Disagree	Leave Blank

7. I frequently give advice to other people.

Strongly Agree	Agree	Don't Know	Disagree	Strongly Disagree	Leave Blank

8. As a general rule, people find their own solutions to their problems.

Strongly Agree	Agree	Don't Know	Disagree	Strongly Disagree	Leave Blank

9. I have had adequate training as a counsellor.

Strongly Agree	Agree	Don't Know	Disagree	Strongly Disagree	Leave Blank

10. I would like to read more about counselling.

Strongly Agree	Agree	Don't Know	Disagree	Strongly Disagree	Leave Blank

11. Most people can benefit from counselling.

Strongly Agree	Agree	Don't Know	Disagree	Strongly Disagree	Leave Blank

12. Counselling should only be practised by trained professionals.

Strongly Agree	Agree	Don't Know	Disagree	Strongly Disagree	Leave Blank

13. I would do more counselling if I had the time.

Strongly Agree	Agree	Don't Know	Disagree	Strongly Disagree	Leave Blank

14. I am a better listener than talker.

Strongly Agree	Agree	Don't Know	Disagree	Strongly Disagree	Leave Blank

15. I am good at confronting other people.

Strongly Agree	Agree	Don't Know	Disagree	Strongly Disagree	Leave Blank

16. Compared with some of my colleagues, I measure up well as a counsellor.

Strongly Agree	Agree	Don't Know	Disagree	Strongly Disagree	Leave Blank

17. I tend to use a particular theoretical model when I counsel.

Strongly Agree	Agree	Don't Know	Disagree	Strongly Disagree	Leave Blank

18. Real counselling skills come from real life experience.

Strongly Agree	Agree	Don't Know	Disagree	Strongly Disagree	Leave Blank

19. Anyone can counsel.

Strongly Agree	Agree	Don't Know	Disagree	Strongly Disagree	Leave Blank

20. I need more practice as a counsellor.

Strongly Agree	Agree	Don't Know	Disagree	Strongly Disagree	Leave Blank

SCORESHEET FOR COUNSELLING-SKILLS ASSESSMENT QUESTIONNAIRE

ITEM	Number who marked 'Strongly Agree'	Number who marked 'Agree'	Number who 'didn't know'	Number who marked 'Disagree	Number who marked 'Strongly Disagree'
1. On the whole, I am a fairly effective counsellor.					
2. I have had a considerable amount of practice as a counsellor.					
3. Given the chance, I would undertake another course in counselling.					
4. I am an effective listener.					
5. As a counsellor, I tend to talk too much.					
6. I use counselling skills every day.					
7. I frequently give advice to other people.					
8. As a general rule, people find their own solutions to their problems.					
9. I have had adequate training as a counsellor.					
10. I would like to read more about counselling.					

ITEM	Number who marked 'Strongly Agree'	Number who marked 'Agree'	Number who 'didn't know'	Number who marked 'Disagree	Number who marked 'Strongly Disagree'
11. Most people can benefit from counselling.					
12. Counselling should only be practised by trained professionals.					
13. I would do more counselling if I had the time.					
14. I am a better listener than talker.					
15. I am good at confronting other people.					
16. Compared to some of my colleagues, I measure up well as a counsellor.					
17. I tend to use a particular theoretical model when I counsel.					
18. Real counselling skills come from real life experience.					
19. Anyone can counsel.					
20. I need more practice as a counsellor.					

HOTSEAT
Activity 72

Time required 45 minutes to 1 hour.

Aim To encourage people to get to know each other better and to practise asking questions in a group setting.

Group size Any number between 5 and 25.

Environment A room in which there is space for everyone to sit in a closed circle of chairs and which is large enough for everyone to pair off and spread out, if required. There should be a flipchart and pad or a white/blackboard and marker pens. This is used to jot down comments from group members during discussion periods. Flipchart sheets containing such comments can be pinned to the wall to act as an *aide mémoire*. These can be kept on the wall until the end of the workshop and they help to maintain continuity of content and demonstrate progress.

You may want to present any theoretical points on an acetate sheet, in which case an overhead projector and screen will be required. Any handouts should be prepared prior to using this activity and it is important that there are enough for each person to have one. Reading lists can be given out at the end of the activity and these should be no more than one page long.

Keep the activity brisk and the discussion lively. Allow everyone to have their say.

Procedure The participants follow these instructions:

- each person has 2 minutes in the 'hotseat';
- while in the hotseat (which may either be their own seat or one placed in the centre of the circle) they can be asked questions, on any subject, by other members of the group;

- any question that a person does not wish to answer may be 'passed';
- after 2 minutes, the person in the hotseat nominates another member of the group to take their place;
- this cycle of events continues until everyone in the group has spent 2 minutes in the hotseat.

Evaluation Two 'rounds' are conducted. In the first round, each person in turn says what they liked *least* about the activity. In the second, each person in turn says what they liked *most* about the activity. The trainer joins in this evaluation process and decides whether or not there is a discussion of the points that are raised.

Closing Participants should be offered a 5-minute period in which to raise questions, express feelings, address particular people in the group or talk through anything else that has arisen from the activity.

SELF-DESCRIPTION
Activity 73

Time required 45 minutes to 1 hour.

Aim To enable trainees to explore their own self-image.

Group size Any number between 5 and 25.

Environment A room in which there is space for everyone to sit in a closed circle of chairs and which is large enough for everyone to pair off and spread out, if required. There should be a flipchart and pad or a white/blackboard and marker pens. This is used to jot down comments from group members during discussion periods. Flipchart sheets containing such comments can be pinned to the wall to act as an *aide mémoire*. These can be kept on the wall until the end of the workshop and they help to maintain continuity of content and demonstrate progress.

You may want to present any theoretical points on an acetate sheet, in which case an overhead projector and screen will be required. Any handouts should be prepared prior to using this activity and it is important that there are enough for each person to have one. Reading lists can be given out at the end of the activity and these should be no more than one page long.

Allow everyone to speak and wait until all thoughts and feelings have been shared in the group before moving on to another activity.

Procedure The group pairs off. Each member of each pair takes it in turn to describe themselves to their partner *in the third person*. Thus, a man may start the description:

> *James Johnson is a man of 34 who is . . .*

The participants describe themselves in this way for a 5-minute period. After 5 minutes, the partners swap roles for a further 5 minutes. The larger group reconvenes and the trainer facilitates a discussion about the activity. The trainer joins in this activity as part of one of the pairs.

Evaluation Each person in turn says what they learnt from the activity and what they will take with them back to 'real life', away from the group.

Closing Participants should be offered a 5-minute period in which to raise questions, express feelings, address particular people in the group or talk through anything else that has arisen from the activity.

QUAKER GROUP
Activity 74

Time required 45 minutes to 1 hour.

Aim To explore a particular style of group decision-making in a counselling-skills workshop.

Group size Any number between 5 and 25.

Environment A room in which there is space for everyone to sit in a closed circle of chairs and which is large enough for everyone to pair off and spread out, if required. There should be a flipchart and pad or a white/blackboard and marker pens. This is used to jot down comments from group members during discussion periods. Flipchart sheets containing such comments can be pinned to the wall to act as an *aide mémoire*. These can be kept on the wall until the end of the workshop and they help to maintain continuity of content and demonstrate progress.

You may want to present any theoretical points on an acetate sheet, in which case an overhead projector and screen will be required. Any handouts should be prepared prior to using this activity and it is important that there are enough for each person to have one. Reading lists can be given out at the end of the activity and these should be no more than one page long.

Allow everyone to speak and wait until all thoughts and feelings have been shared in the group before moving on to another activity.

Procedure This activity is specifically for use as a decision-making enterprise within a counselling-skills workshop. The issue over which a decision needs to be reached is identified. Group participants are then invited to make suggestions as to how the issue may be resolved. Ideas are raised until no further suggestions are floated. Once this has occurred, the last idea that was raised is the one that carries as the decision. Here is an example of this democratic decision making process. The group are trying to solve the question of whether or not there should be a follow-up workshop in addition to the current one.

I propose that we all meet, on a regular basis, every other weekend, perhaps informally . . .

I think we should make do with this workshop. This should be enough for most of us . . .

I propose that we meet at someone's house, in a couple of weeks' time . . .

I suggest that we have a half-day study day in six months' time, once we have had the chance of trying out some of the ideas we have picked up . . .

As no one else speaks after the final contribution, the final suggestion becomes the final decision.

Evaluation The group is divided into pairs and each pair spends 5 minutes discussing what each person liked and disliked about the activity. The group reforms after 5 minutes and an evaluative discussion is held.

Closing Participants should be offered a 5-minute period in which to raise questions, express feelings, address particular people in the group or talk through anything else that has arisen from the activity.

BODY LANGUAGE
Activity 75

Time required 45 minutes to 1 hour.

Aim To explore trainees' use of body language.

Group size Any number between 5 and 25.

Environment A room in which there is space for everyone to sit in a closed circle of chairs and which is large enough for everyone to pair off and spread out, if required. There should be a flipchart and pad or a white/blackboard and marker pens. This is used to jot down comments from group members during discussion periods. Flipchart sheets containing such comments can be pinned to the wall to act as an *aide mémoire*. These can be kept on the wall until the end of the workshop and they help to maintain continuity of content and demonstrate progress.

You may want to present any theoretical points on an acetate sheet, in which case an overhead projector and screen will be required. Any handouts should be prepared prior to using this activity and it is important that there are enough for each person to have one. Reading lists can be given out at the end of the activity and these should be no more than one page long.

Do not hurry people but keep the atmosphere in the group lively and encourage people to share their thoughts and feelings about the activity.

Procedure While it is probably very difficult to generalize about what we are really 'saying' with our body language, it is useful to explore people's perceptions of various sorts of non-verbal communication.

In this activity, the group participants sit, silently, in a circle. A volunteer from the group is then invited to 'arrange' other people in the group, to make them look more comfortable. For example, a group participant may unfold another person's arms, push their shoulders down a little or move their head to one side. After two or three 'arrangements' of this sort, the trainer invites a discussion about how those arrangements looked and felt to all the participants. The trainer takes part in the activity wherever possible.

Evaluation Each person in the group makes notes about what they found useful about the activity. Then an evaluative discussion is held with the trainer as facilitator of that discussion.

Closing Participants should be offered a 5-minute period in which to raise questions, express feelings, address particular people in the group or talk through anything else that has arisen from the activity.

SENTENCE COMPLETION
Activity 76

Time required 45 minutes to 1 hour.

Aim To explore trainees' views of a range of issues relating to self-awareness and counselling.

Group size Any number between 5 and 25.

Environment A room in which there is space for everyone to sit in a closed circle of chairs and which is large enough for everyone to pair off and spread out, if required. There should be a flipchart and pad or a white/blackboard and marker pens. This is used to jot down comments from group members during discussion periods. Flipchart sheets containing such comments can be pinned to the wall to act as an *aide mémoire*. These can be kept on the wall until the end of the workshop and they help to maintain continuity of content and demonstrate progress.

You may want to present any theoretical points on an acetate sheet, in which case an overhead projector and screen will be required. Any handouts should be prepared prior to using this activity and it is important that there are enough for each person to have one. Reading lists can be given out at the end of the activity and these should be no more than one page long.

Keep the activity brisk and the discussion lively. Allow everyone to have their say.

Procedure The trainer uses the following list of incomplete statements and invites each person, in turn, to complete one, either working systematically through the list or choosing statements at random. The incomplete statements are:

- A good counsellor always ...
- The most important rule in counselling is ...

- The thing I would most like to change about myself is . . .
- The person most similar to me in this group is . . .
- The person who is most different to me is . . .
- The next stage in my counselling-skills training includes . . .
- I would most like to . . .
- If I could live anywhere I would choose to live . . .
- If I could change places with someone that everyone here knows, it would be . . .
- My greatest asset is . . .
- Counselling calls for . . .
- The best counsellors always . . .
- The most difficult thing for me is . . .
- The things I most like are . . .
- The people I admire are . . .

The trainer may choose to add to this list of incomplete statements. At the end of one or more 'rounds' the group discusses the outcome of the activity.

Evaluation Two 'rounds' are conducted. In the first round, each person in turn says what they liked *least* about the activity. In the second, each person in turn says what they liked *most* about the activity. The trainer joins in this evaluation process and decides whether or not there is a discussion of the points that are raised.

Closing Participants should be offered a 5-minute period in which to raise questions, express feelings, address particular people in the group or talk through anything else that has arisen from the activity.

CENTRING
Activity 77

Time required 45 minutes to 1 hour.

Aim To explore the concepts of centring.

Group size Any number between 5 and 25.

Environment A room in which there is space for everyone to sit in a closed circle of chairs and which is large enough for everyone to pair off and spread out, if required. There should be a flipchart and pad or a white/blackboard and marker pens. This is used to jot down comments from group members during discussion periods. Flipchart sheets containing such comments can be pinned to the wall to act as an *aide mémoire*. These can be kept on the wall until the end of the workshop and they help to maintain continuity of content and demonstrate progress.

You may want to present any theoretical points on an acetate sheet, in which case an overhead projector and screen will be required. Any handouts should be prepared prior to using this activity and it is important that there are enough for each person to have one. Reading lists can be given out at the end of the activity and these should be no more than one page long.

Keep the activity brisk and the discussion lively. Allow everyone to have their say.

Procedure The idea of 'centring' involves feeling contained, comfortable with yourself and not 'thrown' by the other person. It is said to be an important element in counselling. To be centred is to be in control of yourself, to feel that you are not being manipulated by the other person, nor particularly uncomfortable in their presence.

For this activity, group members pair off. They sit opposite each other, with their eyes closed. They are encouraged to take stock of themselves, take some deep breaths and concentrate on settling down. It is then suggested that as they begin to feel more *centred*, they open their eyes and meet the gaze of their partner. If they find themselves uncomfortable, of somehow thrown off-centre by the other person, they close their eyes again and re-gather themselves. This activity continues until both parties in each pair are comfortable sitting quietly with their partners.

The trainer invites the larger group to reconvene. Then, a discussion is held about the activity. Two facets are discussed: the *process* of the activity (what it felt like to do it) and the *content* (what was talked about during the activity). As always, the process is more important than the content and, sometimes, the trainer may choose to discuss *only* the process. Also, the trainer helps the group to identify ways in which what has been learnt from the activity can be related to the group members' professional or personal life. The group trainer joins in the activity wherever possible.

Evaluation Each person in turn says what they learnt from the activity and what they will take with them back to 'real life', away from the group.

Closing Participants should be offered a 5-minute period in which to raise questions, express feelings, address particular people in the group or talk through anything else that has arisen from the activity.

SUSTAINED EYE CONTACT

Activity 78

Time required 45 minutes to 1 hour.

Aim To encourage trainees to explore eye contact.

Group size Any number between 5 and 25.

Environment A room in which there is space for everyone to sit in a closed circle of chairs and which is large enough for everyone to pair off and spread out, if required. There should be a flipchart and pad or a white/blackboard and marker pens. This is used to jot down comments from group members during discussion periods. Flipchart sheets containing such comments can be pinned to the wall to act as an *aide mémoire*. These can be kept on the wall until the end of the workshop and they help to maintain continuity of content and demonstrate progress.

You may want to present any theoretical points on an acetate sheet, in which case an overhead projector and screen will be required. Any handouts should be prepared prior to using this activity and it is important that there are enough for each person to have one. Reading lists can be given out at the end of the activity and these should be no more than one page long.

Allow everyone to speak and wait until all thoughts and feelings have been shared in the group before moving on to another activity.

Procedure This is a variation on the children's game. The group pairs off and each pair sits facing each other, in silence. Then, their task is to sit making sustained eye contact with each other. Participants should note the point at which such sustained gazing is broken.

An alternative to this activity is to allow partners to talk to each other while they make sustained eye contact.

The trainer invites the larger group to reconvene. Then, a discussion is held about the activity. Two facets are discussed: the *process* of the activity (what it felt like to do it) and the *content* (what was talked about during the activity). As always, the process is more important than the content and, sometimes, the trainer may choose to discuss *only* the process. Also, the trainer helps the group to identify ways in which what has been learnt from the activity can be related to the group members' professional or personal life. The group trainer joins in the activity wherever possible.

Evaluation The group is divided into pairs and each pair spends 5 minutes discussing what each person liked and disliked about the activity. The group reforms after 5 minutes and an evaluative discussion is held.

Closing Participants should be offered a 5-minute period in which to raise questions, express feelings, address particular people in the group or talk through anything else that has arisen from the activity.

FUTURE
Activity 79

Time required 45 minutes to 1 hour.

Aim To explore trainees' plans for the future.

Group size Any number between 5 and 25.

Environment A room in which there is space for everyone to sit in a closed circle of chairs and which is large enough for everyone to pair off and spread out, if required. There should be a flipchart and pad or a white/blackboard and marker pens. This is used to jot down comments from group members during discussion periods. Flipchart sheets containing such comments can be pinned to the wall to act as an *aide mémoire*. These can be kept on the wall until the end of the workshop and they help to maintain continuity of content and demonstrate progress.

You may want to present any theoretical points on an acetate sheet, in which case an overhead projector and screen will be required. Any handouts should be prepared prior to using this activity and it is important that there are enough for each person to have one. Reading lists can be given out at the end of the activity and these should be no more than one page long.

Encourage everyone to discuss the activity afterwards and make sure that everyone who wants to say something gets the chance.

Procedure This activity is aimed at helping group members to identify what they need to do, in terms of counselling skills, in the future. The activity is useful towards the end of a counselling-skills workshop.

The group pairs off. One member of each pair talks through what plans they have made to develop their own counselling skills. The following headings can be used:

- Plans in terms of everyday life.
- Plans in terms of more training.
- Plans in terms of personal development.

After 5 minutes, the pairs swap roles and the other member of the pair relates their plans for the future. This activity is *not* a conversation but a structured pairs activity. The group trainer joins in the activity wherever possible.

After the second 5-minute period the group reconvenes and a discussion is held about future plans. The trainer also focuses on how the group members *feel* about their developmental plans.

Evaluation Each person in the group makes notes about what they found useful about the activity. Then an evaluative discussion is held with the trainer as facilitator of that discussion.

Closing Participants should be offered a 5-minute period in which to raise questions, express feelings, address particular people in the group or talk through anything else that has arisen from the activity.

CLARIFYING COUNSELLING

Activity 80

Time required 2–4 hours.

Aim To explore all aspects of counselling.

Group size Any number between 5 and 25.

Environment A room in which there is space for everyone to sit in a closed circle of chairs and which is large enough for everyone to pair off and spread out, if required. There should be a flipchart and pad or a white/blackboard and marker pens. This is used to jot down comments from group members during discussion periods. Flipchart sheets containing such comments can be pinned to the wall to act as an *aide mémoire*. These can be kept on the wall until the end of the workshop and they help to maintain continuity of content and demonstrate progress.

You may want to present any theoretical points on an acetate sheet, in which case an overhead projector and screen will be required. Any handouts should be prepared prior to using this activity and it is important that there are enough for each person to have one. Reading lists can be given out at the end of the activity and these should be no more than one page long.

Do not hurry people but keep the atmosphere in the group lively and encourage people to share their thoughts and feelings about the activity.

Procedure The group divides into pairs. One of each pair is nominated 'counsellor' to the other's 'client'. The counsellors then use all the counselling skills they have learnt to help the 'client' to talk through everything *they* know about counselling. Thus, counselling skills are used to explore all aspects of counselling. This activity can be run for up to 1 hour. After the designated period, the pairs swap roles and the activity is run again.

After the second designated period, the larger group reconvenes and a discussion about all aspects of counselling is developed. Enough time should be taken to enable all trainees to talk about the aspects of counselling that they are still puzzled by, or about which they still have concerns. This activity can be used on the last afternoon of a counselling skills workshop. The trainer takes part in the activity wherever possible.

Evaluation Two 'rounds' are conducted. In the first round, each person in turn says what they liked *least* about the activity. In the second, each person in turn says what they liked *most* about the activity. The trainer joins in this evaluation process and decides whether or not there is a discussion of the points that are raised.

Closing Participants should be offered a 5-minute period in which to raise questions, express feelings, address particular people in the group or talk through anything else that has arisen from the activity.

TOPICS FOR DISCUSSION

A number of the activities call for trainees to discuss topics of their choice. Sometimes, such topics can be hard to think of on the spur of the moment. Here is a list of possible topics:

- Childhood
- Old age
- Maturity
- Counselling problems
- Counselling skills
- Counselling theory
- Difficulties at work
- Problems at home
- Holidays
- Musical tastes
- My theory of the universe
- Views on management
- The best things about this workshop
- The worst things about this workshop
- The present government
- Where I would go if I could go anywhere in the world
- My past
- How I would like things to be in the future
- How I deal with my own anger
- How I cope with stress
- How I cope with other people's stress
- Feminism
- Homosexuality
- Previous training
- School/college/university
- What I want to achieve
- My greatest achievement to date
- Parents
- Abortion
- The Law
- The Church

- Coping with difficult people
- Saying 'no'
- Signing contracts
- Starting a business
- Working for yourself
- The organization I work for
- The organization I would like to work for
- Changes I would make
- Places I would like to visit
- Places I would like to live
- Places I have visited
- Selling a house
- Buying a car
- Writing
- Public speaking
- Arguments
- Difficulties in relationships
- Working with young people
- Working with the elderly
- Reaching middle age
- Leaving school
- Going to university
- Studying at home

References

Berne, E. (1972) *What Do You Say After You Say Hello?* Corgi, London.

Branscombe, M. (1991) 'The Data Protection Act: What You Need to Know', *PC Answers*: 1(3), 56-7.

Burnard, P. (1989) *Counselling Skills for Health Professionals*, Chapman & Hall, London.

(1991) *Learning Human Skills* (2nd edn), Butterworth-Heinemann, Oxford.

(1992) *Experiential Learning in Action*, Avebury, Aldershot.

Cox, M. (1990) *Structuring the Therapeutic Process*, Jessica Kingsley, London.

Egan, G. (1990) *The Skilled Helper* (4th edn), Brooks/Cole, Pacific Grove, CA.

Fiedler, F.E. (1950) 'The Concept of an Ideal Therapeutic Relationship', *Journal of Consulting Psychology* 14, 239-45.

Gendlin, E. (1981) *Focusing*, Bantam, New York.

Hall, C. (1954) *A Primer of Freudian Psychology*, Mentor, New York.

Heron, J. (1975) *Six Category Intervention Analysis*, Human Potential Research Project, University of Surrey, Guildford.

(1977) *Dimensions of Facilitator Style*, Human Potential Research Project, University of Surrey, Guildford.

(1990) *Helping the Client*, Sage, London.

Jarvis, P. (1986) *Adult Learning in the Social Context*, Croom Helm, London.

Kelly, G. (1955) *The Psychology of Personal Constructs* (2 vols), Norton, New York.

(1969) 'The Autobiography of a Theory', in B. Mahrer (ed) *Clinical Psychology and Personality: the Selected Papers of George Kelly*, Wiley, New York.

Knowles, M. (1990) *The Adult Learner: A Neglected Species* (3rd edn), Gulf, TX.

Maslach, C. (1981) *Burnout: the cost of caring*, Prentice Hall, Englewood Cliffs, NJ.

Masson, J. (1990) *Against Therapy*, Pan, London.

Nelson-Jones, R. (1981) *The Theory and Practice of Counselling Psychology*, Holt, Rinehart & Winston, London.

(1984) *Personal Responsibility: Counselling and Therapy: An Integrative Approach*, Harper & Row, London.

Perls, F. (1969) *Gestalt Therapy Verbatim*, Real People Press, Moab, UT.

Pines, A.M., Aronson, E. and Kafry, D. (1981) *Burnout: from tedium to personal growth*, Free Press, New York.

Rogers, C.R. (1952) *Client-Centred Counselling*, Constable, London.

(1957) 'The Necessary and Sufficient Qualities of Therapeutic and Personality Change', *Journal of Consulting Psychology* 21, 95–104.

(1967) *On Becoming a Person*, Constable, London.

Sartre, J.-P. (1955) *Being and Nothingness*, Philosophical Library, New York.

Truax, R. (1967) *Towards Effective Counselling and Psychotherapy*, Aldine, New York.

de Unamuno, M. (1954) *Tragic Sense of Life*, Dover, New York.

Van Durzen Smith, E. (1989) *Existential Counselling in Practice*, Sage, London.

Bibliography

Adler, R. and Rodman, G. (1988) *Understanding Human Communication* (3rd edn), Holt, Rinehart & Winston, New York.

Adler, R.B., Rosenfield, L.B. and Towne, N. (1983) *Interplay: The Process of Interpersonal Communication*, Holt, Rinehart & Winston, London.

Alberti, R. (ed) (1977) *Assertiveness, Innovations, Applications, Issues*, Impact, San Luis Obispo, CA.

Alberti, R.E. and Emmons, M.L. (1982) *Your Perfect Right: A Guide to Assertive Living* (4th edn), Impact, San Luis Obispo, CA.

Allan, D.M.E., Grosswald, S.J. and Means, R.P. (1984) 'Facilitating Self-Directed Learning', in J.S. Green, S.J. Grosswald, E. Suter and D.B. Walthall (eds), *Continuing Education for the Health Professions*, Jossey Bass, San Francisco.

Allan, J. (1989) *How to Develop Your Personal Management Skills*, Kogan Page, London.

Argyle, M. (1983) *The Psychology of Interpersonal Behaviour* (4th edn), Penguin, Harmondsworth.

Argyle, M (ed) (1981) *Social Skills and Health*, Methuen, London.

Argyris, C. (1982) *Reasoning, Learning and Action*, Jossey Bass, San Francisco.

Argyris, C. and Schon, D. (1974) *Theory in Practice: Increasing Professional Effectiveness*, Jossey Bass, San Francisco.

Arnold, E. and Boggs, K. (1989) *Interpersonal Relationships: Professional Communication Skills for Nurses*, Saunders, Philadelphia.

Atwood, A.H. (1979) 'The Mentor in Clinical Practice', *Nursing Outlook* 27, 714–17.

Ausberger, D. (1979) *Anger and Assertiveness in Pastoral Care*, Fortress Press, Philadelphia.

Baer, J. (1976) *How to be Assertive (Not Aggressive): Women in Life, in Love and on the Job*, Signet, New York.

Bannister, D. and Fransella, F. (1986) *Inquiring Man* (3rd edn), Croom Helm, London.

Baruth, L.G. (1987) *An Introduction to the Counselling Profession*, Prentice Hall, Englewood Cliffs, NJ.

Belkin, G.S. (1984) *Introduction to Counselling*, Brown, Dubuque, IA.

Bellack, A.S. and Hersen, M. (eds) (1979) *Research and Practice in Social Skills Training*, Plenum Press, New York.

Benner, P. and Wrubel, J. (1989) *The Primacy of Caring: Stress and Coping in Health and Illness*, Addison Wesley, Menlo Park, CA.

Bolger, A.W. (ed) (1982) *Counselling in Britain: A Reader*, Batsford Academic, London.

Bond, M. and Kilty, J. (1986) *Practical Methods of Dealing With Stress* (2nd edn), Human Potential Research Project, University of Surrey, Guildford.

Boone, E.J., Shearon, R.W., White, E.E. *et al* (1980) *Serving Personal and Community Needs Through Adult Education*, Jossey Bass, San Francisco.

Boud, D. (ed) (1973) *Experiential Learning Techniques in Higher Education*, Human Potential Learning Project, University of Surrey, Guildford.

Boud, D.J. (ed) (1981) *Developing Student Autonomy in Learning*, Kogan Page, London.

Boud, D., Keogh, R. and Walker, M. (1985) *Reflection: Turning Experience into Learning*, Kogan Page, London.

Boud, D. and Prosser, M.T. (1980) 'Sharing Responsibility; Staff–Student Cooperation in Learning', *British Journal of Educational Technology* 11(1), 24–35.

Bower, S.A. and Bower, G.H. (1976) *Asserting Yourself*, Addison Wesley, Reading, MA.

Boydel, E.M. and Fales, A.W. (1983) 'Reflective Learning; Key to Learning From Experience', *Journal of Humanistic Psychology* 23(2), 99–117.

Brandes, D. and Phillips, R. (1984) *The Gamester's Handbook, Vol 2*, Hutchinson, London.

Brasweel, M. and Seay, T. (1984) *Approaches to Counselling and Psychotherapy*, Waverly, Prospect Heights.

Brookfield, S.D. (1986) *Understanding and Facilitating Adult Learning: A Comprehensive Analysis of Principles and Effective Practices*, Open University Press, Milton Keynes.

(1987) *Developing Critical Thinkers: Challenging Adults to Explore Alternative Ways of Thinking and Acting*, Open University Press, Milton Keynes.

Broome, A. (1990) *Managing Change*, Macmillan, London.

Brown, A. (1979) *Groupwork*, Heinemann, London.

Brown, D. and Srebalus, D. J. (1988) *An Introduction to the Counselling Process*, Prentice Hall, Philadelphia.

Brown, S.D. and Lent, R.W. (eds) (1984) *Handbook of Counselling Psychology*, Wiley, Chichester.

Brundage, D.H. and Mackeracher, D. (1980) *Adult Learning Principles and their Application to Program Planning*, Ministry of Education, Ontario.

Buber, M. (1958) *I and Thou*, Scribner's, New York.

(1966) *The Knowledge of Man: A Philosophy of the Interhuman* (ed M. Freidman, trans R.G. Smith), Harper & Row, New York.

Bugental, E.K. and Bugental, J.F.T. (1984) 'Dispiritedness: A New Perspective on a Familiar State', *Journal of Humanistic Psychology*, 24(1), 49–67.

Burnard, P. (1983) 'Through Experience and From Experience', *Nursing Mirror* 156(9), 29–33.

(1988) 'The Journal of an Assessment and Evaluation Tool in Nurse Education', *Nurse Education Today*, 8, 105–7.

(1989) *Counselling Skills for Health Professionals*, Chapman & Hall, London.

(1989) 'Developing Critical Ability in Nurse Education', *Nurse Education Today* 9, 271–5.

(1989) 'Existentialism as a Theoretical Basis for Counselling in Psychiatric Nursing', *Archives of Psychiatric Nursing* III(3), 142–7.

(1989)'Experiential Learning and Andragogy – Negotiated Learning in Nurse Education, a Critical Appraisal', *Nurse Education Today* 9(5), 300–306.

(1989) 'Exploring Nurse Educators' Views of Experiential Learning, a Pilot Study', *Nurse Education Today* 9(1), 39–45.

(1989) *Teaching Interpersonal Skills: A Handbook of Experiential Learning for Health Professionals*, Chapman & Hall, London.

(1990) 'Ambivalence in Humanistic Psychology; Self and Society', *European Journal of Humanistic Psychology* XVIII(3), 40–41.

(1990) 'Is Anyone Here a Mentor?', *Nursing Standard* 4(37), 46.

(1990) *Learning Human Skills: An Experiential Guide for Nurses* (2nd edn), Heinemann, London.

(1990) 'Meaningful Dialogue', in R.L. Ismeurt, E.N. Arnold and V.B. Carson (1990) *Readings in Concepts Fundamental to Nursing*, Springhouse, PA.

(1990) 'Recording Counselling in Nursing', *Senior Nurse* 10(3), 26–7.

(1990) 'Stating the Case, Counselling', *Journal of the British Association for Counselling* 1(4), 114–16.

(1990) 'The Student Experience: Adult Learning and Mentorship Revisited', *Nurse Education Today* (10(5), 349–53.

(1990) 'The Supervisory Role', *Journal of District Nursing* (July), 26–7.

(1991) 'Assertiveness and Clinical Practice', *Nursing Standard* 5(33), 37–9.

(1991) *Coping With Stress in the Health Professions: A Practical Guide*, Chapman & Hall, London.

(1991) 'Exploring Personal Values', *Journal of District Nursing* 9(7), 7–8.

(1991) 'Improving Through Reflection', *Journal of District Nursing* 9(11), 10–12.

(1991) 'Interpersonal Skills Training', *Journal of District Nursing* 9(10), 17–20.

(1991) *Learning From Experience: Experiential Learning in Action*, Avebury/Gower, Aldershot.

(1991) 'Peer Support Groups', *Journal of District Nursing* 9(8), 19–20.

(1991) 'Perceptions of Experiential Learning', *Nursing Times* 87(8), 47.

(1991) 'Using Video as a Reflective Tool in Interpersonal Skills Training', *Nurse Education Today* 11, 143–6.

(1992) *Communication in the Caring Professions: Communication Skills for the Support Worker in the Health Professions*, Edward Arnold, London.

(1992) *Effective Communication in the Health Professions*, Chapman & Hall, London.

Burnard, P. and Morrison, P. (1989) 'What is an Interpersonally Skilled Person? A Repertory Grid Account of Professional Nurses' Views', *Nurse Education Today* 9(6), 384–91.

(1990) *Nursing Research in Action: Developing Basic Skills*, Macmillan, London.

(1990) 'Counselling Attitudes in Health Visiting Students', *Health Visitor* 63(11), 389–90.

(1991) 'Nurses' Interpersonal Skills: A Study of Nurses' Perceptions', *Nurse Education Today* 11(1), 24–9.

Calnan, J. (1983) *Talking With Patients*, Heinemann, London.

Campbell, A. (1984) *Paid to Care?*, SPCK, London.

(1984) *Moderated Love*, SPCK, London.

Campbell, A.V. (1981) *Rediscovering Pastoral Care*, Darton, Longman & Todd, London.

Carkuff, R.R. (1969) *Helping and Human Relations: Vol I, Selection and Training*, Holt, Rinehart & Winston, New York.

Carlisle, J. and Leary, M. (1982) 'Negotiating Groups', in R. Payne and C. Cooper (eds) *Groups at Work*, Wiley, Chichester.

Carson B.V. (1989) *Spiritual Dimensions of Nursing Practice*, W.B. Saunders, Philadelphia.

Charles, J. (1983) 'When Carers Crash', *Social Work Today*, 15(12), 18–20.

Chene, A. (1983) 'The Concept of Autonomy in Adult Education; A Philosophical Discussion', *Adult Education Quarterly*, 32(1), 38–47.

Chenevert, M. (1978) *Special Techniques in Assertiveness Training for Women in the Health Professions*, C.V. Mosby, St Louis.

Clark, C. (1978) *Assertive Skills for Nurses*, Contemporary Publishing, Wakefield, MA.

Clark M. (1978) 'Meeting the Needs of the Adult Learner; Using Non-Formal Education for Social Action', *Convergence* XI, 3–4.

Claxton, G. (1984) *Live and Learn: An Introduction to the Psychology of Growth and Change in Everyday Life*, Harper & Row, London.

Clutterbuck, D. (1985) *Everybody Needs a Mentor: How to Further Talent Within an Organisation*, The Institute of Personnel Management, London.

Collins, G.C. and Scott, P. (1979) 'Everyone Who Makes It Has a Mentor', *Harvard Business Review* 56, 89–101.

Corey, F. (1983) *I Never Knew I Had A Choice* (2nd edn), Brooks/Cole, CA.

Cormier, L.S. (1987) *The Professional Counsellor: A Process Guide to Helping*, Prentice Hall, Englewood Cliffs, NJ.

Corsini, R. (1984) *Current Psychotherapies* (3rd edn), Peacock, Itasca, IL.

Cunningham, P.M. (1983) 'Helping Students Extract Meaning from Experience', in R.M. Smith (ed) *Helping Adults Learn How to Learn* (New Directions for Continuing Education No 19), Jossey Bass, San Francisco.

Curran, J. and Monti, P. (eds), *Social Skills Training: A Practical Handbook for Assessment and Treatment*, Guildford, New York.

Curtis, L., Sturm, G., Billing, D.R. and Anderson, J.D. (1989) 'At the Breaking Point; When Should An Overworked Nurse Bail Out?', *Journal of Christian Nursing* 6(1), 4–9.

Daleo, R.E. (1986) 'Taking Care of the Caregivers; Five Strategies for Stamina', *American Journal of Hospice Care* 3(5), 33–38.

Daniels, V. and Horowitz, L.J. (1984) *Being and Caring: A Psychology for Living* (2nd edn), Mayfield, Mountain View, CA.

Dawley, H. and Wenrich, W. (1976) *Achieving Assertive Behaviour: A Guide to Assertive Training*, Brooks/Cole, Monterey, CA.

de Bono, E. (1982) *de Bono's Thinking Course*, BBC, London.

De Vito, J.A. (1986) *The Interpersonal Communication Book* (4th edn), Harper & Row, New York.

Deckard, G.J. (1989) 'Impact of Role Stress on Physical Therapists' Emotional and Physical Well-Being', *Physical Therapist* 69(9), 713–18.

Dewe, P.J. (1989) 'Stressor Frequency, Tension, Tiredness and Coping; Some Measurement Issues and a Comparison Across Nursing Groups', *Journal of Advanced Nursing* 14(4), 308–20.

Dickson, A. (1985) *A Woman in Your Own Right: Assertiveness and You*, Quartet Books, London.

Dixon, D.N. and Glover, J.A. (1984) *Counselling: A Problem Solving Approach*, Wiley, Chichester.

Dolan, N. (1987) 'The Relationship Between Burnout and Job Satisfaction in Nurses', *Journal of Advanced Nursing* 12(1), 3–12.

Doswell, W.M. (1989) 'Physiological Responses to Stress', *Annual Review of Nursing Research* 7, 51–69.

Douglas, T. (1976) *Groupwork Practice*, Tavistock, London.

Dowd, C. (1983) 'Learning Through Experience', *Nursing Times* (27 July), 50–52.

Downe, S. (1989) 'Prophets Without Honour – The Burn-Out of Midwifery Visionaries', *Midwives Chronicle* 102(1214), 93–4.

Dryden, W., Charles-Edwards, D. and Woolfe, R. (1989) *Handbook of Counselling in Britain*, Routledge, London.

Duncan, S. and Fiske, D.W. (1977) *Face-to-Face Interaction: Research, Methods and Theory*, Lawrence Erlbaum, Hillsdale, NJ.

Edmunds, M. (1983) 'The Nurse Preceptor Role', *Nurse Practitioner* 8(6), 52–3.

Egan, G. (1986) *Exercises in Helping Skills* (3rd edn), Brooks/Cole, Monterey, CA.

Ellis, A. (1962) *Reason and Emotion in Psychotherapy*, Lyle, Stuart, NJ.

Ellis R. and Whittington, D. (1981) *A Guide to Social Skill Training*, Croom Helm, London.

Ellis, R. and Whittington, D. (eds) (1983), *New Directions in Social Skills Training*, Croom Helm, London.

Epting, F. (1984) *Personal Construct Counselling and Psychotherapy*, Wiley, Chichester.

Ernst, S. and Goodison, L. (1981) *In our Own Hands: a Book of Self Help Therapy*, The Womens' Press, London.

Evans, D. (ed) (1990) *Why Should We Care?*, Macmillan, London.

Everly, G.S. and Rosenfeld, R. (1981) *The Nature and Treatment of the Stress Response: A Practical Guide for Clinicians*, Plenum Press, New York.

Fabry, J. (1968) *The Pursuit of Meaning*, Beacon Press, Boston, MA.

Fagan, M.M. and Walter, G. (1982) 'Mentoring Among Teachers', *Journal of Educational Research* 76(2), 113–18.

Fay, A. (1978) *Making Things Better By Making Them Worse*, Hawthorne, New York.

Feldenkrais, M. (1972) *Awareness Through Movement*, Harper & Row, New York.

Fernando, S. (1990) *Mental Health, Race and Culture*, Macmillan, London.

Ferruci, P. (1982) *What We May Be*, Turnstone Press, Wellingborough.

Filley, A.C. (1975) *Interpersonal Conflict Resolution*, Scott, Foresman, Glenview, IL.

Fineman, S. (1985) *Social Work Stress and Intervention*, Gower, London.

Firth, H., McKeown, P., McIntee, J. and Britton, P. (1987) 'Burn-Out, Personality and Support in Long-Stay Nursing', *Nursing Times* 83(32), 55–7.

Firth, J. (1985) 'Personal Meanings of Occupational Stress; Cases from the Clinic', *Journal of Occupational Psychology* 58, 139–48.

Firth, J.A. (1986) 'Levels and Sources of Stress in Medical Students', *British Medical Journal* 292, 1177–80.

Fisher, R. and Ury, W. (1983) *Getting to Yes: Negotiating Agreement Without Giving In*, Hutchinson, London.

Fisher, S. (1986) *Stress and Strategy*, Lawrence Erlbaum, London.

Fisher, S. and Reason, J. (1988) *Handbook of Life: Stress, Cognition and Health*, Wiley, Chichester.

Foggo-Pays, E. (1983) *An Introductory Guide to Counselling*, Ravenswood, Beckenham.

Fontana, D. (1989) *Managing Stress*, British Psychological Society and Routledge, London.

Fordham, F. (1966) *An Introduction to Jung's Psychology*, Penguin, Harmondsworth.

Francis, D. and Young, D. (1979) *Improving Work Groups: A Practical Manual for Team Building*, University Associates, San Diego, CA.

Frankl, V.E. (1959) *Man's Search for Meaning*, Beacon Press, New York.

(1960) 'Paradoxical Intention: A Logotherapeutic Technique', *American Journal of Psychotherapy* 14, 520–35.

(1969) *The Will to Meaning*, World Publishing Co, New York.

(1975) *The Unconscious God*, Simon & Schuster, New York.

(1975) 'Paradoxical Intention and Dereflection; A Logotherapeutic Technique', *Psychotherapy, Theory, Research and Practice* 12(3), 226–37.

(1978) *The Unheard Cry for Meaning*, Simon & Schuster, New York.

Freeman, R. (1982) *Mastering Study Skills*, Macmillan, London.

French, P. (1983) *Social Skills for Nursing Practice*, Croom Helm, London.

Freudenberger, H. and Richelson, G. (1974) *Burnout: How to Beat the High Cost of Success*, Bantam, New York.

Fromm, E. (1941) *Escape from Freedom*, Avon, New York.

Geller, L. (1985) 'Another Look at Self-Actualisation', *Journal of Humanistic Psychology* 24(2), 93–106.

Gendlin, E.T. and Beebe, J. (1968) 'An Experiential Approach to Group

Therapy', *Journal of Research and Developments in Education* 1, 19-29.

George, P. and Kummerow, J. (1981) 'Mentoring for Career Women', *Training* 18(2), 44-9.

Gibbs, G. (1981) *Teaching Students To Learn*, Open University, Milton Keynes.

Gibson, R.L. and Mitchell, M.H. (1986) *Introduction to Counselling and Guidance*, Collier Macmillan, London.

Gilleard, C.J. (1987) 'Influence of Emotional Distress Among Supporters on the Outcome of Psychogeriatric Day Care', *British Journal of Psychiatry* 150, 219-23.

Glennerster, H. and Owens, P. (1990) *Nursing in Conflict*, Macmillan, London.

Goffman, I. (1971) *The Presentation of Self in Everyday Life*, Penguin, Harmondsworth.

Goldberg, L and Beznitz, S. (1982) *Handbook of Stress, Theoretical and Clinical Aspects*, Macmillan, New York.

Gordon, S. and Waldo, M. (1984) 'The Effects of Assertive Training on Couples' Relationships', *American Journal of Family Therapy* 12, 73-7.

Gormally, J. (1982) 'Evaluation of Assertiveness, Effects of Gender, Rater Involvement and Level of Assertiveness', *Behaviour Therapy* 13, 219-25.

Graham, N.M. (1988) 'Psychological Stress as a Public Health Problem; How Much Do We Know?', *Community Health Studies* 12(2), 151-60.

Haggerty, L.A. (1987) 'An Analysis of Senior Nursing Students' Immediate Responses to Distressed Patients', *Journal of Advanced Nursing* 12(4), 451-61.

Halmos, P. (1965) *The Faith of the Counsellors*, Constable, London.

Hanks, L, Belliston, L. and Edwards, D. (1977) *Design Yourself*, Kaufmann, Los Altos, CA.

Hanson, P. (1986) *The Joy of Stress*, Pan, London.

Hargie, O. (ed) (1987) *A Handbook of Communication Skills*, Croom Helm, London.

Hargie, O., Saunders, C. and Dickson, D. (1981) *Social Skills in Interpersonal Communication* (2nd edn), Croom Helm, London.

Harris, T. (1969) *I'm OK, You're OK*, Harper & Row, London.

Hawkins, P. and Shohet, R. (1989) *Supervision and the Helping Professions*, Open University Press, Milton Keynes.

Health Education Authority, High Stress Occupation Working Party (1988) *Stress in the Public Sector: Nurses, Police, Social Workers and Teachers*, Health Education Authority.

Heginbotham, C. (1990) *Mental Health, Human Rights and Legislation*, Macmillan, London.

Heins, M., Fahey, S.N. and Leiden, L.I. (1984) 'Perceived Stress in Medical, Law and Graduate Students', *Journal of Medical Education* 59, 169–79.

Herinck, R. (ed) (1980) *The Psychotherapy Handbook*, New American Library, New York.

Heron, J. (1973) *Experiential Training Techniques*, Human Potential Research Project, University of Surrey, Guildford.

(1977) *Catharsis in Human Development*, Human Potential Research Project, University of Surrey, Guildford.

(1977) *Behaviour Analysis in Education and Training*, Human Potential Research Project, University of Surrey, Guildford.

(1978) *Co-Counselling Teachers' Manual*, Human Potential Research Project, University of Surrey, Guildford.

(1980) *Paradigm Papers*, Human Potential Research Project, University of Surrey, Guildford.

Heywood-Jones, I. (1989) *Helping Hands*, Macmillan, London.

(1990) *The Nurse's Code: A Practical Approach to the Code of Professional Conduct*, Macmillan, London.

Hill, S.S. and Howlett, H.A. (1988) *Success in Practical Nursing in Personal Vocational Issues*, W.B. Saunders, Philadelphia.

Hingley, P. and Cooper, C.L. (1986) *Stress and the Nurse Manager*, Wiley, Chichester.

Howard, G.S., Nance, D.W. and Meyers, P. (1987) *Adaptive Counselling and Therapy: A Systematic Approach to Selecting Effective Treatments*, Jossey Bass, San Francisco.

Hughes, J. (1987) *Cancer and Emotion*, Wiley, Chichester.

Hull, D. and Schroeder, H. (1979) 'Some Interpersonal Effects of Assertion, Non-Assertion and Aggression', *Behaviour Therapy* 10, 20–9.

Hurding, R.F. (1985) *Roots and Shoots, A Guide to Counselling and Psychotherapy*, Hodder & Stoughton, London.

Hutchins, D.E. (1987) *Helping Relationships and Strategies*, Brooks/Cole, Monterey, CA.

Ivey, A.E. (1987) *Counselling and Psychotherapy: Skills, Theories and Practice*, Prentice Hall International, London.

Jacobson, D. (1989) 'Context and the Sociological Study of Stress: An Invited Response to Pearlin', *Journal of Health and Social Behaviour* 30(3), 257–60.

James, M. and Jongeward, D. (1971) *Born to Win: Transactional Analysis with Gestalt Experiments*, Addison Wesley, Reading, MA.

Jenkins, E. (1987) *Facilitating Self-Awareness: A Learning Package*

Combining Group Work with Computer Assisted Learning, Open Software Library, Wigan.

Jenkins, J.F. and Ostchega, Y. (1986) 'Evaluation of Burnout in Oncology Nurses', *Cancer Nursing* 9(3), 108–16.

Johnson, D.W. (1972) *Reaching Out*, Prentice Hall, Englewood Cliffs, NJ.

Johnson, D.W. and Johnson, F.P. (1982) *Joining Together* (2nd edn), Prentice Hall, Englewood Cliffs, NJ.

Jones, G. (1988) 'High-Tech Stress; Identification and Prevention', *Occupational Health*, 40(9), 648–9.

Jones, J.G., Janman, K., Payne, R.L. and Rick, J.T. (1987) 'Some Determinants of Stress in Psychiatric Nurses', *International Journal of Nursing Studies* 24(2), 129–44.

Jourard, S. (1964) *The Transparent Self*, Van Nostrand, Princeton, NJ.
    (1971) *Self-Disclosure: An Experimental Analysis of the Transparent Self*, Wiley, New York.

Jung, C.G. (1976) *Modern Man in Search of a Soul*, Routledge & Kegan Paul, London.

Kavanagh, K.H. (1989) 'Nurses' Networks, Obstacles and Challenge', *Archives of Psychiatric Nursing* 3(4), 226–33.

Keller, K.L. and Koenig, W.J. (1989) 'Sources of Stress and Satisfaction in Emergency Practice', *Journal of Emergency Medicine* 7(3), 293–9.

Kelly, C. (1979) *Assertion Training: A Facilitator's Guide*, University Associates, La Jolla, CA.

Kennedy, E. (1979) *On Becoming a Counsellor*, Gill and Macmillan, London.

Kilty, J. (1978) *Self and Peer Assessment*, Human Potential Research Project, University of Surrey, Guildford.
    (1987) *Staff Development for Nurse Education, Practitioners Supporting Students: A Report of a 5-Day Development Workshop*, Human Potential Research Project, University of Surrey, Guildford.

King, E.C. (1984) *Effective Education in Nursing: A Guide to Teaching and Assessment*, Aspen, MD.

Kizer, W.M. (1987) *The Health Workplace: A Blueprint for Corporate Action*, Delmar, London.

Knowles, M. (1978) *The Adult Learner, A Neglected Species* (2nd edn), Gulf, TX.
    (1980) *The Modern Practice of Adult Education: From Pedagogy to Andragogy*, 2nd edn, Follett, Chicago.

Knowles M. S. *et al* (1984) *Andragogy in Action: Applying Modern Principles of Adult Learning*, Jossey Bass, San Francisco.

Knox, A.B. (ed) (1980) *Teaching Adults Effectively*, Jossey Bass, San Francisco.

Koberg, D. and Bagnal, J. (1981) *The Revised All New Universal Traveller: A Soft-Systems Guide to Creativity, Problem-Solving and the Process of Reaching Goals*, Kaufmann, Los Altos, CA.

Kopp, S. (1974) *If You Meet the Buddha on the Road, Kill Him!, A Modern Pilgrimage Through Myth, Legend and Psychotherapy*, Sheldon Press, London.

Kottler, J.A. and Brown, R.W. (1985) *Introduction to Therapeutic Counselling*, Brooks/Cole, Monterey, CA.

L'Abate, L. and Milan, M. (eds) (1985) *Handbook of Social Skills Training and Research*, Wiley, New York.

Lachman, V.D. (1983) *Stress Management: A Manual for Nurses*, Grune and Stratton, Orlando, FL.

Lang, A.J. and Jakubowski, P. (1978) *The Assertive Option*, Research Press, Champaign, IL.

Larson, D.G. (1986) 'Developing Effective Hospice Staff Support Groups; Pilot Test of an Innovative Training Program', *Hospice Journal* 2(2), 41–55.

Lazarus, R.S. and Folkman, S. (1984) *Stress, Appraising and Coping*, Springer, New York.

Leady, N.K. (1989) 'A Physiological Analysis of Stress and Chronic Illness', *Journal of Advanced Nursing* 14(10), 868–76.

Leech, K. (1986) *Spirituality and Pastoral Care*, Sheldon Press, London.

Lewis, H. and Streitfield, H. (1971) *Growth Games*, Bantam, New York.

Lewis, M. (1987) *Writing to Win*, McGraw-Hill, London.

Liberman, R.P., King, L.W., De Risi, W.J. and McCann, M. (1976) *Personal Effectiveness*, Research Press, Champaign, IL.

Luft, J. (1984) *Group Processes: An Introduction to Group Dynamics* (2nd edn), Mayfield, San Francisco.

Marcer, D. (1986) *Biofeedback and Related Therapies in Clinical Practice*, Chapman & Hall, London.

Marshall, E.K. and Kurtz, P.D. (eds) (1982) *Interpersonal Helping Skills: A guide to Training Methods, Programs and Resources*, Jossey Bass, San Francisco.

Marson, S. (ed) (1990) *Managing People*, Macmillan, London.

May, K.M. *et al* (1982) 'Mentorship for Scholarliness; Opportunities and Dilemmas', *Nursing Outlook* 30, 22–8.

McGuire, J. and Priestley, P. (1981) *Life After School: A Social Skills Curriculum*, Pergamon, Oxford.

McIntee, J. and Firth, H. (1984) 'How to Beat the Burnout', *Health and Social Services Journal* (9th February), 166–8.

Meichenbaum, D. (1979) *Cognitive Behaviour Modification: An Integrative Approach*, Plenum Press, New York.

Meichembaum, D. and Jaremko, M.E. (1983) *Stress Reduction and Prevention*, Plenum Press, New York.

Merriam, S. (1984) 'Mentors and Protégés; A Critical Review of the Literature', *Adult Education Quarterly* 33(3), 161–73.

Meyeroff, M. (1972) *On Caring*, Harper & Row, New York.

Mezeiro, J. (1981) 'A Critical Theory of Adult Learning and Education', *Adult Education* 32(1), 3–24.

Michelson, L., Sugari, D., Wood, R. and Kazadin, A. (1983) *Social Skills Assessment and Training with Children*, Plenum Press, New York.

Middleton, J.F. (1989) 'Modifying the Behaviour of Doctors and Their Receptionists in Recurrent Stressful Activity', *Journal of the Royal College of General Practitioners* 39, 62–4.

Milne, D., Burdett, C. and Beckett, J. (1986) 'Assessing and Reducing the Stress and Strain of Psychiatric Nursing', *Nursing Times* 82(19), 59–62.

Moore, D. (1977) *Assertive Behaviour Training, An Annotated Bibliography*, Impact, San Luis Obispo, CA.

Moreno, J.L. (1959) *Psychodrama, Vol II*, Beacon House Press, Beacon, NY.

(1969) *Psychodrama, Vol III*, Beacon House Press, Beacon, NY.

(1977) *Psychodrama, Vol I* (4th edn), Beacon House Press, Beacon, NY.

(1987) 'Negotiating and Bargaining', in O. Hargie (ed) *A Handbook of Communication Skills*, Croom Helm, London.

Morley, I.E. (1982) 'Preparation for Negotiating L Conflict, Commitment and Choice', in H. Bradstatter, J.H. Davis and G. Stocker-Kreichgauer (eds) *Group Decision Making*, Academic Press, London.

Morrison, P. and Burnard, P. (1990) 'Interpersonal Skills; A Smallest Space Analysis', *Nursing Times* 86(14), 55.

Morsund, J. (1985) *The Process of Counselling and Therapy*, Prentice Hall, Englewood Cliffs, NJ.

Munro, A., Manthei, B. and Small, J. (1988) *Counselling: The Skills of Problem-Solving*, Routledge, London.

Murgatroyd, S. (1986) *Counselling and Helping*, British Psychological Society and Methuen, London.

Murgatroyd, S. and Woolfe, R. (1982) *Coping with Crisis-Understanding and Helping Persons in Need*, Harper & Row, London.

Myerscough, P.R. (1989) *Talking With Patients; A Basic Clinical Skill*, Oxford Medical Publications, Oxford.

Nadler, L. (ed) (1984) *The Handbook of Human Resource Development*, Wiley, New York.

Nash, E.S. (1989) 'Occupational Stress and the Oncology Nurse', *Nursing* 4(8), 37–8.

Nelson, M.J. (1989) *Managing Health Professionals*, Chapman & Hall, London.

Nelson-Jones, R. (1981) *The Theory and Practice of Counselling Psychology*, Holt, Rinehart & Winston, London.

(1983) *Practical Counselling Skills: A Psychological Skills Approach for the Helping Professions and for Voluntary Counsellors*, Holt, Rinehart & Winston, London.

(1984) *Personal Responsibility, Counselling and Therapy: An Integrative Approach*, Harper & Row, London.

(1988) *Practical Counselling and Helping Skills: Helping Clients to Help Themselves*, Cassell, London.

Nichols, K. and Jenkinson, J. (1990) *Leading a Support Group*, Chapman & Hall, London.

Nierenberg, G.I. (1973) *Fundamentals of Negotiation*, Hawthorn, New York.

Ohlsen, A.M., Horne, A.M. and Lawe, C.F. (1988) *Group Counselling*, Holt, Rinehart & Winston, New York.

Open University Coping With Crisis Group (1987) *Running Workshops: A Guide for Trainers in the Helping Professions*, Croom Helm, London.

Osborn, S.M. and Harris, G.G. (1975) *Assertive Training for Women*, Charles C. Thomas, Springfield, IL.

Palmer, M.E. and Deck, E.S. (1982) 'Assertiveness Education; One Method for Teaching Staff and Patients', *Nurse Educator* (Winter), 36–9.

Payne, R. and Firth-Conzens, J. (eds) (1987) *Stress in Health Professionals*, Wiley, Chichester.

Peplau, H.E. (1988) *Interpersonal Relationships in Nursing*, Macmillan, London.

Phelps, S. and Austin, N. (1975) *The Assertive Woman*, Impact, San Luis Obispo, CA.

Phillip-Jones, L. (1982) *Mentors and Protégés*, Arbour House, New York.

(1983) 'Establishing a Formalised Mentoring Programme', *Training and Development Journal* (February), 38–42.

Pope, B. (1986) *Social Skills Training for Psychiatric Nurses*, Harper & Row, London.

Porritt, L. (1990) *Interaction Strategies: An Introduction for Health Professionals* (2nd edn), Churchill Livingstone, Edinburgh.

Postman, N. and Weingartner, C.W. (1969) *Teaching as a Subversive Activity*, Penguin, Harmondsworth.

Priestley, P., McQuire, J., Flegg, D., Hemsley, V. and Welham, D. (1978) *Social Skills and Personal Problem Solving*, Tavistock, London.

Roche, G.R. (1979) 'Much Ado About Mentors', *Harvard Business Review*, 56, 14–28.

Rogers, C.R. (1983) *Freedom to Learn for the Eighties*, Merrill, Columbus, OH.

(1985) 'Toward a More Human Science of the Person', *Journal of Humanistic Psychology* 25(4), 7–24.

Rogers, C.R. and Stevens, B. (1967) *Person to Person: The Problem of Being Human*, Real People Press, Lafayette, CA.

Rogers, J.C. (1982) 'Sponsorship – Developing Leaders for Occupational Therapy', *American Journal of Occupational Therapy* 36, 309–13.

Rogers, J.C. and Dodson, S.C. (1988) 'Burnout in Occupational Therapists', *American Journal of Occupational Therapy* 42(12), 787–92.

Rowan, J. (1986) 'Holistic Listening', *Journal of Humanistic Psychology* 26(1), 83–102.

Roy, I. (1973) *Structural Integration*, Viking Press, New York.

Russell, P. (1979) *The Brain Book*, Routledge & Kegan Paul, London.

Scammell, B. (1990) *Communication Skills*, Macmillan, London.

Schafer, B.P. and Morgan, M.K. (1980) 'An Experiential Learning Laboratory; A New Dimension in Teaching Mental Health Skills', *Issues in Mental Health Nursing* 2(3), 47–57.

Schon, D.A. (1983) *The Reflective Practitioner: How Professionals Think in Action*, Basic Books, New York.

Schorr, T.M. (1978) 'The Lost Art of Mentoring', *American Journal of Nursing* 78, 1873.

Schulman, D. (1982) *Intervention in Human Services, A guide to skills and knowledge* (3rd edn), C.V. Mosby, St Louis.

Scott, W.P. (1981) *The Skills of Negotiating*, Gower, Aldershot.

(1986) *The Skills of Communicating*, Gower, Aldershot.

Shafer, P. (1978) *Humanistic Psychology*, Prentice Hall, Englewood Cliffs, NJ.

Shamian, J. and Inhaber, R. (1985) 'The Concept and Practice of Preceptorship in Contemporary Nursing; A Review of Pertinent Literature', *International Journal of Nursing Studies* 22(2), 79–88.

Shaw, M.E. (1981) *Group Dynamics: The Psychology of Small Group Behaviour*, McGraw-Hill, New York.

Shostak, A.B. (1980) *Blue-Collar Stress*, Addison Wesley, Reading, MA.

Shropshire, C.O. (1981) 'Group Experiential Learning in Adult Education', *Journal of Continuing Education in Nursing* 12(6), 5–9.

Simon, S.B., Howe, L.W. and Kirschenbaum, H. (1978) *Values Clarification* (Revised edition), A & W Visual Library, New York.

Smith, E. and Wilks, N. (1988) *Meditation*, Macdonald, London.

Strauss, A. (1978) *Negotiations: Varieties, Contexts and Social Order*, Jossey Bass, San Francisco.

Sudman, S. and Bradburn, N.M. (1982) *Asking Questions: A Practical*

Guide to Questionnaire Design, Jossey Bass, San Francisco.

Tanner, D. (1986) *That's Not What I Meant! How Conversational Style Makes or Breaks Your Relations With Others*, Dent, London.

Taubman, B. (1976) *How to Become an Assertive Woman*, Simon & Schuster, New York.

Taylor, E. (1988) 'Anger Intervention', *American Journal of Occupational Therapy* 42(3), 147–55.

Torrington, D. (1982) *Face-To-Face in Management*, Prentice Hall, Englewood Cliffs, NJ.

Totton, N. and Edmonston, E. (1988) *Reichian Growth Work: Melting the Blocks to Life and Love*, Prism Press, Bridport.

Tough, A.M. (1982) *Intentional Changes; A Fresh Approach to Helping People Change*, Cambridge, New York.

Trower, P. (ed) (1984) *Radical Approaches to Social Skills Training*, Croom Helm, London.

Trower, P., Bryant, B.M. and Argyle, M. (eds) *Social Skills and Mental Health*, Methuen, London.

Trower, P., O'Mahony, J.M. and Dryden, W. (1982) 'Cognitive aspects of social failure; Some Implications for Social Skills Training', *British Journal of Guidance and Counselling* 10, 176–84.

Tschudin, V. (1986) *Counselling Skills for Nurses*, Bailliere Tindall, London.

Tschudin, V. and Schober, J. (1990) *Managing Yourself*, Macmillan, London.

Vredenburgh, D.J. and Trinkaus, R.J. (1983) 'An Analysis of Role Stress Among Hospital Nurses', *Journal of Vocational Behaviour* 22, 82–95.

Wallace, W.A. (1986) *Theories of Counselling and Psychotherapy: A Basic Issues Approach*, Allyn and Bacon, Boston, MA.

Wheeler, D.D. and Janis, I.L. (1980) *A Practical Guide for Making Decisions*, Free Press, New York.

Whitaker, D.S. (1985) *Using Groups to Help People*, Tavistock/Routledge, London.

Wilkinson, J, and Canter, S. (1982) *Social Skills Training Manual: Assessment, Programme Design and Management of Training*, Wiley, Chichester.

Winn, M.F. (1988) 'Imagery and the School Nurse', *Journal of School Health* 58(3), 112–14.

Wlodkowski, R.J. (1985) *Enhancing Adult Motivation to Learn*, Jossey Bass, San Francisco.

Woodward, J. (1988) *Understanding Ourselves: The Uses of Therapy*, Macmillan, London.

Zajonc, R. (1980) 'Feelings and Thinking, Preferences Need No Interference', *American Psychologist* 35, 151–75.

Zander, A. (1982) *Making Groups Effective*, Jossey Bass, San Francisco.
Zastrow, C. (1984) 'Understanding and Preventing Burnout', *British Journal of Social Work* 14, 141–55.

Index of Activities

Index